# The Freedom Funnel

## Real Talk for Real Estate Agents

## Paul Curtis

*"The Money We Possess Is The Instrument Of Liberty"*
*—Rousseau*

# Contents

# Preface

You didn't get a real estate license to get a job working nights and weekends. You were/are looking for a viable business that creates freedom. When we're honest with ourselves, we know that isn't what we got. We got nights and weekends and chasing the next deal. That's because we never learned how to systematically build a business that delivers that freedom.

This book is the real talk truth of what it takes to create that viable business. It's built from the streets of Metro Detroit — not Malibu or Manhattan. The promises here are real world for real people. The Freedom Funnel will challenge you regarding your inner life, and it will equip you for external success. This system will help you have the business you want and the life you envision.

This book is not the get rich quick scheme of infomercials and webinars. This isn't the promise of sports cars, mansions and vacations because of a system that several people you don't know and never heard of swear worked for them. It isn't hype. It isn't short term. It is real talk for real estate agents.

Here is the conceptual framework that will help you make sense of it once and for all. The Freedom Funnel is a system for you, the residential agent, to help you build the real estate business you envision and create your desired destiny. This system is written specifically for you, the real estate professional, by a real estate professional.

After 16 years of non-profit community development work, and 12 years of teaching at local colleges, Tina and I started a career in real estate. We became the #1 listing team for Keller Williams in the Great Lakes Region. We were listed as Top Agents in The Wall Street Journal. But I learned a lot of life lessons the hard way through all of that. Top of that list is that it isn't how much you make, but how much you keep and what it cost you to get it that matters. I also learned how incredibly hard it is to be successful for the long haul. It's one thing to become successful and quite another to remain that way.

Now, at Red Door, we are proud to help people with such a significant part of their lives as their housing. And at this stage of my life I'm especially happy to help our agents reach their goals in business and to do it in a way that allows them to thrive as people at the same time. We all (yes, you too) have something to offer our communities. We have the best lives when we get to help others have good lives. Real estate allows us to do just that when we do it right. This book is about how to do it right!

You'll have to win with your strengths and not let your weaknesses beat you. That means you'll have to face the real talk truth of who you are and who you are not, and choose to be who you know you can be. There's freedom in these pages if, and only if, you'll do what it takes to make it happen. That's why *"The Real Talk Truths"* are followed by the *"Watcha Gonna Do?"* action points. I'm pulling for you. I'm your new fan because I know what kind of courage it takes to face the truth and choose to be free.

The first part of this book is about you and what it takes to be your best. There is no system in the world that will work if you will not work it. Be patient and read it all. Don't rush yourself and miss the initial point of working on you. Dealing with your self is the first to do item. Don't take that as an insult. It's just *Real Talk Truth #1*.

# Introduction

The world changed, and not for the better. The demise of the middle class is well documented. Flattened wages with cost of living increases, a system of commerce that favors the wealthy and a recent global economic collapse have created the most inequitable distribution of wealth since the roaring 20's. Only the richest among us have seen income increases. That has happened while productivity has increased significantly. We work harder for less. The reality is that you and I, and almost everyone we will ever serve in real estate, are way more stressed out than we used to be.

When I was a kid in the factory town of Flint Michigan, I saw the same bumper sticker on the back of all the Buick sedans and Chevy pick-up trucks around town. It had the logo of the UAW and simply read, "30 and Out." It was the slogan of the factory worker who had a great paying job, a pension plan, health care, sick leave, paid vacation and early retirement. As long as you showed up on time and performed, you were going to be just fine. One household worker could take care of themselves, their spouse, their kids, and put those kids through college! The UAW factory workers, and workers all over the country, were firmly middle class. Not anymore.

Today most of us are living paycheck to paycheck. In fact, more than 50 percent of us are a month of lost wages away from financial ruin. That's a far cry from the traditional definition of the middle class:

able to be without income for a full year without changing your circumstance. Today many of us are working a second job and dropping Little Caesar's pizza on the table for our kids. We're poisoning them slowly with cheap/bad food. While we're doing that, we as a people in Michigan happen to be subsidizing that particular billionaire's next huge venture. Here in Detroit, Little Caesar's former owner, the late Mike Illitch (RIP) also owned the Detroit Red Wings and the Detroit Tigers. The Illitch Holdings' new District Detroit was built for the Red Wings (the Pistons will play there too) in a 40+ block area with retail, housing, entertainment, etc. using, in part, our hard earned tax dollars!

It connects the dots of his empire and cements his legacy. South of I-75 and on the iconic corridor of Woodward Avenue sits Comerica Park (home of the Detroit Tigers) and the Fox Theater (the grandest of all entertainment venues in Detroit) both of which are owned by Mr. Illitch's heirs. Northwest of that sits the Motor City Casino (a very profitable gambling/entertainment facility) also owned by Mr. Illitch's heirs. In between them sat some of the worst slums in America for decades. But now the people have built one of the grandest single developments in Detroit's history to the tune of hundreds of millions of dollars in public and pseudo public monies so the Illitch family can pull off the biggest business move of their lives.

Remember, we're doing that on our way to our second job. We're doing that while we are working to try to keep our heads above water, feed our kids and maybe pay down our student debt finally so we can buy a house. Forget about vacations, sick leave, pensions, or affording to send our kids to college. We're doing this while we are absent as parents and our kids are being raised by the internet and one another.

Sound bleak? Well, it is bleak. The radio show we started in 2013 is called Michigan Real Talk. It is in that voice I write this book. No punches pulled—just real talk. It is in that bleak context that we seek to be real estate professionals. Most of us are running like mad to try to stay afloat ourselves. Two years ago every real estate license in the state had to be renewed. Roughly one third of them didn't renew!

I get it. The world is a moving sidewalk in the wrong direction for us economically. It's really hard. The popular narrative in response is "work harder, run faster, do more." On the one hand, there is no way we can. Americans work way more than we used to. On the other hand, we have no choice. We have to hustle to keep up.

Speaking of real talk, let me tell you something else. You have the power to change the game, to flip the script. You don't have to live this way. You can find freedom and lead many, many others to it too. What you are reading now can give you the knowledge to change your life. It is a blueprint to help you build and own your American Dream. Much of it you already know. But that old phrase, "knowledge is power" isn't true. Knowledge is necessary, but not sufficient, as it relates to power. The real talk truth of it is that knowledge correctly applied is power. Hard work and dedication pay off!

So it is for many of us in real estate these days. We have some knowledge, but not enough. And we have no real sense of how to consistently apply it in fruitful ways. So we run. We chase the next deal and never build a business that leads to freedom. In fact, we become stuck in a job and we're dependent on the ebb and flow of the economy rather than in charge of our fate. Believe me I know this from personal experience. The Freedom Funnel can be your key to changing that if, and only if, you will read and apply.

# Section 1

# The Story

# Chapter 1
# Why We Do What We Do?

*"Men are chiefly creatures of action" –David Hume*

The phone rang on a Wednesday morning about 10:20. It was my then 21 year old daughter. Her words stopped my heart and chilled my soul, "I'm at the Police Station. I've been arrested because I've been using heroin." That's a call you don't ever want. There's only one worse, and thank God it wasn't that call. At least I was hearing her voice. I dropped everything, jumped into action and as of the writing of this, she's doing well.

That was about 7 years after I lost my home to foreclosure during the housing collapse. Losing a home when you have five kids is traumatic. It didn't help that the family dog needed to be put down at the same time. That happened six or so years after a divorce and in the midst of a global meltdown. So when I write about knowing the pain of working like a dog and getting paid like a puppy, I know what I'm talking about. When I say I understand that scrambling to get deals done and not being there for your kids is a miserable existence, I've lived it.

Maybe it's not a good idea to tell you how much I've screwed up in my life. Maybe I should just tell you the upside. I've been a Platinum Producer, the #1 listing agent in my region and Tina (my wife) and

I were named as part of the Top 250 Agents in the country in The Wall Street Journal. But so what? It's not what you make that counts. It's what you keep, and what it cost you to get it. My kids are too high a price to pay for any of it. My pride as a man and a father is too costly. My freedom to be the person I know I am deep down and do the things I want to do and have the life I want to have is what really matters. I bet that's what matters to you too. I know what it is to not be that, to not do that and to not have that. I bet you do too.

But I also know what it is to turn the corner and have the freedom to be there for my kids and to travel to places I always wanted to go (I'm editing this page from New Zealand). I also know what it is to be a volunteer in my community making a difference in people's lives. That's the result of The Freedom Funnel. What it has done for me, it can do for you. So why don't we do it already?

*Real Talk Truth: We know most of what we need to know, and if we'd act on it consistently, we'd learn most of the rest along the way. But we often don't until we absolutely have to and even then we might not.*

*Watcha Gonna Do? Take a minute and write down what you already know you should be doing that you're not doing. Then identify the most important thing and circle it on the list. I say list because you and I both know, if we're honest with ourselves, there are several things we know we should be doing that we are not.*

# Chapter 2
# Underhand Free Throws

I once heard Rick Barry interviewed on NPR. For those that don't know, Rick Barry was an All-Star basketball player who is in the Hall of Fame and was, in 1996, named one of the All Time 50 Greatest Players in NBA history. He was a fierce competitor. They say he was the sort of teammate that was difficult sometimes because he demanded your best at all times.

He scored over 25,000 professional points in 14 seasons. More than 18,000 of those 25,000 were in the NBA and the rest in the ABA. He won championships in both leagues and was named the NBA Finals MVP. But one of the things he was best known for was his underhand free throws. Yep, granny style. When he retired, he was the all-time leader in percentage of free throws made at .900! One season he missed only nine attempts all year.

Barry was the son of a coach and his dad got him to try the technique. He tells the story of being coached to shoot that way because it is way more consistent. You can reproduce the movement when you're tired or under pressure at any time. But he told his dad/coach that he didn't want to do it because people would make fun of him. His dad's answer was, "they can't make fun of you if you're making them." Well sure enough, Barry heard fans at an away game talking. The first was shouting something meant to embarrass Barry, but the second told that fan loud enough for Barry to hear, "what are you making fun of him for? He makes his shots."

In 4 years of college and 14 years of professional basketball, Rick Barry shot free throws granny style and made them. He played when Wilt Chamberlain played. Wilt was a notoriously bad free throw shooter. His overall game made him a dominant player. In fact, he is the only player in history to score 100 points in a game. But as his career developed, opposing teams developed the strategy of fouling him rather than letting him shoot because he made a measly 51% of his free throws. The same strategy became famous as Hack-a-Shaq when it was applied to Shaquille O'Neal. Shaq was the most dominant center to play in his era. But his career made free throw percentage was only 53%.

Today, in Detroit, we have one of the most athletic young centers in the league in Andre Drummond. In his first four years he shot only 38% from the free throw line. It is so bad that the coach has to pull him out of the game towards the end because the other team just fouls him no matter where on the court he is or who on the team has the ball. It's a good strategy for them because he will miss nearly two out of three times from the free throw line!

Barry worked with many players in the off season to teach them to shoot free throws under hand. Almost no one would do it in front of anyone during the games when shots counted. Chamberlain told him he was unwilling to look like that in public. Shaq wouldn't change either. If Chamberlain would have shot just 75% from the line, he would have scored an additional 2,839 points in his career! But he didn't because he wouldn't. Barry was only able to persuade one player to change to the under hand shot. That was a player you never heard of even if you are a fan of the NBA. But that player increased his free throw percentage from under 50% to 80% in two years.

The point to this free throw talk is that there are things you know would work to increase your business that you don't do. You know systematically calling through your sphere of influence will make a tremendous difference, but you don't. There are reasons you don't. One of my reasons was that I feel funny about it. All the trainers I ever had told me I had to call and "ask for the business". I didn't want to be that guy. So I was the guy that was busy chasing deals when I should have been home with my kids. The Freedom Funnel has cures for these kinds of sticking points if you'll do it. What are you not accomplishing? It's probably not because you can't. It's probably because you won't!

*Real Talk Truth: We all have things, like the underhand free throw, that we don't want to do. But there are ways to do them that aren't as painful as we think.*

*Watcha Gonna Do? Pick the scariest things about your business and write them out. Tell yourself the truth about what holds you back. It's just between you and you at this point.*

# Chapter 3
# On Behavior

David Hume (Scottish philosopher 1711-1776) was primarily interested in the question of why we do what we do? As it relates to the above story, why would Wilt, Shaq and now Andre Drummond not engage in a behavior that would increase their success? Why did they not increase their productivity and help their teams win? Hume's perspective interests me.

He was part of The Empiricist Movement that understood humans as chiefly creatures of action. The Empiricists introduced us to the idea of *tabula rasa* which is a Latin phrase meaning blank slate. It is the idea that we are all born like a blank canvas or a clean white board. What we end up doing with our lives is the result of what gets written, drawn, erased, rewritten and redrawn on that white board. Hume suggested we do what we do because of our experiences, sentiments, ideas, beliefs and passions.

When I taught this to my philosophy students I drew a long line (like a time line) across a huge white board and wrote the words *tabula rasa* at the left end of it and said we are all born a blank slate. Near the start, I drew about 8 or 9 hash marks, top to bottom, intersecting the line and wrote the word "events" because we're born a blank slate, but events happen in our lives and draw on our existence. The next word I wrote was "sentiments" because we have things happen and we have feelings about those things before we have thoughts about them. We are humans. We feel fast and think slow. The next word on the line is "ideas." But notice that the ideas we have about life come after the sentiments and feelings we have about what happens in our lives! This is a very important point. As humans, we feel fast and think slow.

It was at this point I asked the class if anyone had a food that they think of as repulsive? Of course we all do, and there is almost always an event and sentiments clearly attached to that idea of repulsive food. One of my children would bring up roasted vegetables and an event at a cafeteria in a day camp in Colorado. But one of my philosophy students brought up mashed potatoes! The whole class gasped because mashed potatoes rock! So I asked the young guy, "Dude, what happened?" I just knew there had to be a story that included an event and feelings that led this poor young man to the idea that mashed potatoes were repulsive. His answer was short and oh so clear. He said, "when I was little, someone held out a spoon of mashed potatoes and asked me, 'do you want some ice cream?'" Uh-huh, that would do it. Not only would it be about the taste and texture, but the humiliation as that jerk laughed at the expression on this youngster's face. Don't you hate mean people?

My story is about roasted marshmallows. I know, I know, roasted marshmallows are awesome, but there was an event. I was 8 years old. My parents were separated for about two years at this point. My mother did what all divorcing parents do. She decided I needed to know her side of the family better. We were broke and without a car. Her mom sent two one way train tickets so we could get out to Salt Lake City and drive an old Ford Falcon they had back to Michigan. I grew up in Flint, Michigan (at roughly sea level) and didn't know any of my extended family. Apparently I had cousins who lived in and around Salt Lake City (4200 feet above sea level).

When we flew in we went straight to my uncle's house (4,400 feet above sea level). He was taking my cousins camping. Now, when you live in Salt Lake City and go camping, you go camping in the mountains. My mom was thrilled and we jumped into a pick-up truck and drove up to 9,500 feet above sea level to camp.

Please understand I know nothing about camping at this point. I am a city kid. In fact, I'm an inner-city kid to be more precise. People that slept in tents were homeless in my experience. I was way out of my element.

I also was extremely competitive. When I found out I had boy cousins, I was sizing them up immediately. When I found out you could have pine cone fights, I was all in! I knew about snow ball fights. We even had dirt clod fights in the summer (I told you we were poor). But pine cone fights were a revelation. I was ecstatic. In no time I was hopping over logs, ducking behind trees, running at full speed and throwing on the run. I was a whirlwind of activity— at nearly 10,000 feet above sea level. Up until that day I had spent my entire life at about 100 feet above sea level. It wasn't long before my chest was burning, my head was pounding and I was suffering from altitude sickness.

But we were camping, so someone lit a fire and someone else brought out marshmallows. I knew what marshmallows were. My eyes immediately zeroed in on that bag of sugar, and it wasn't long before I was stuffing my face with roasted, melted sugar! Do you know what happens when you add sugar to altitude sickness and headache? I don't have an uncle Ralph or an uncle Earl, but I was behind a tree calling for both of them. I was so sick. My mother figured it out and had my uncle drive me down to the valley so I could start to feel better. But the idea of roasted marshmallows as a yummy treat was a distant memory by then. Not only did I get painfully and violently sick while eating them, it was also connected to the break-up of my parents and the embarrassment of not being able to hang with my cousins. To this day, when people want to make s'mores, I usually just ask for a small piece of the chocolate bar and skip the rest.

# Chapter 4
# Some Ideas are Challenged, Some are Reinforced

The point to that disgusting story above is to illustrate that our ideas are formed on the other side of events and sentiments. Our ideas are not stand alone concepts and they don't occur to us in a vacuum. They are colored with the good, the bad and the ugly of life, and it doesn't ever stop. Events continue to occur in our lives. Events that we have sentiments about. Those events and sentiments sometimes reinforce ideas we have, but sometimes they challenge and change ideas we have. The ideas we have that get reinforced develop into beliefs.

Beliefs clearly differ from ideas. They are harder to change. We begin to order our lives around beliefs. But even some beliefs can be challenged and changed. Some events and sentiments are so strong they can shake our beliefs. For instance, I believed that girl in high school loved me — until I saw her with that other boy. Ouch.

The beliefs that get reinforced become our passions. It's these passions that we act on. We act when events touch our passions and require action. Apparently, Wilt, Shaq and Andre Drummond were satisfied with poor performance from the free throw line. Apparently, they feared what shooting free throws granny style looked like more than they longed to score points for their team. Maybe they are more passionate about looking good than being good at free throws. Often, Drummond isn't even allowed in the game when the game is on the line because of it.

I submit to you that the game is on the line for you right now. It starts to cut deep when you realize that there are things you should be doing that you are not doing. There are things you could do that would free up your life and allow you to live out your passions. There are things within your power that would change the lives of those you love for the better. But you don't do them. You continue to not take control and order your life the way it needs to be ordered to make it what you want it to be.

Believe me, I know from personal experience. I spent much of my real estate life doing what I call the 1,3,1,3,1,3,4 dance. That comes from my interpretation of the excellent work of Stephen Covey way back in 1989. He laid out a quadrant where square 1 is those activities that are urgent and important, square 2 activities are important but not urgent, square 3 activities are urgent and unimportant and square 4 activities are neither urgent nor important. I spent my life in the 1,3,1,3,1,3,4 dance. Because of the tyranny of the urgent, I was unable to discern between the important and unimportant until I collapsed into quadrant 4 in front of a TV. Meanwhile the important but not urgent things were too often left undone.

## Four Quadrants of Activities

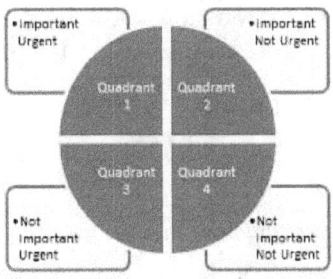

Quadrant 2 activities are the ones that change your life for the better. In regards to your health they are things like eating right and regular exercise. They are important, but not urgent (until they are). With relationships they are things like spending significant time with people and dealing honestly with whatever issues there are instead of sweeping them under the rug. Under the rug they trip you up later. In business they are the activities that produce a viable business for the long haul. But they are things that get set aside for the tyranny of the urgent. Can you relate?

I assure you, I jumped into action when I received the call from my daughter that she was under arrest because she had been using heroin. I was in action non-stop. It was urgent and important. I was in action because my kids are what I am most passionate about. Here's the thing — I was passionate about my kids way before I reordered my life in such a way as to live out my passion. It took having my world rocked over and over in traumatic ways to finally do it. It took the pain and fear of possibly losing my kid to jail or worse to get off my ass and make the changes. It took them suffering to make me man up. That's a damn shame. I was telling myself that I was doing what I had to do to keep everyone taken care of, but I wasn't there enough to give them everything they needed. They needed me not just the money I was making. That's the real talk truth of it.

So why was I not doing what I needed to do? Part of it was knowledge, but most of it was more insidious than that. And if you're really honest with yourself, most of what is holding you back is more about your internal struggles than your external circumstances. If you are anything at all like me (and since we're both humans I bet you are), you already know most of what you need to know. It's about behaviors not knowledge. It's about consistently doing what you already know you should be doing. It's about habits.

So Why Don't You? That's a complicated question with layers of answers, but take a look at a simple answer. I had a philosophy professor that said, "there's a simplicity on the far side of complexity that is worth your right arm." I believe Professor Moreland was right about that. I believe there is a simple enough view of these things that applies meaningfully to all of us. I believe understanding it is one of the keys to your freedom.

We are all motivated by security and significance. We're motivated by success (significance) and by being loved and cared for (security). Some of us are motivated more by significance and some more by security. Some of us are motivated by feeling successful and some by feeling lovable. Some of us want to be successful and significant so we feel lovable and secure in that love. Whatever the combination, what operates deep down inside of us is fairly simple. Why and how that's what is operating in us can be very complicated, but I'm not writing to psychoanalyze you. I'm writing to help you get to where you are consistently taking the actions that will make your life better.

I know what your struggle is like. I've worked side by side with hundreds of agents and cooperated with over a thousand on transactions. I know what it is to work long days and long weeks and long months year after year and have very little to show for it. This is about your freedom. This about you having the tools and blueprints you need to build the life you want. This is about you being the person you've always suspected you could be because deep down you know your best self is awesome! In this book is the system and strategy to finally put it all together. Keep reading and create your desired destiny.

*Real Talk Truth: Your best you is awesome. But your less than best you keeps getting in your way.*

*Whatcha Gonna Do? Take the time to write what you know to be true about being your best you in your business. What would you be doing consistently to make your business and your life better if you were allowing your best you to run your business?*

# Chapter 5
# Know Thyself

*"The unexamined life is not worth living"* –Socrates

People that don't stop to consider and contemplate their lives end up being led around by others and often without even noticing. At best they end up proclaiming the sort of victory the barn yard marksman claimed. You know about him don't you? He's the one that took his rifle outside and shot three holes in the side of his barn. Then he painted bullseyes around the holes so he could proclaim himself an expert marksman. I've never been in any shooting contests, but I'm pretty sure that's not how it works. And in life you need to understand the target or goal before you take your shots because if you aim at nothing you're sure to hit it every time. You need to understand what you need to do to get what you want to have. First you need to be your best self to consistently live it out.

To understand yourself, you need to recognize that your behaviors are the product of your thoughts and feelings. You do what you do because of the years of conditioning that have developed your beliefs and core beliefs about yourself, the world and others. Wilt and Shaq shot free throws poorly because of their feelings and thoughts about themselves, the world and others. We run after real estate business instead of building a business that runs with or without us because of our feelings and thoughts about ourselves, the world and others.

Cognitive Behavioral Therapists talk about the triangle that connects our actions, feelings and thoughts. Imagine a triangle with your actions at the top point, your feelings at the bottom right point and your thoughts at the bottom left point. But now imagine the lines connecting those points are all double sided arrows indicating that your thoughts influence your feelings while your feelings equally influence your thoughts. It's a two way street. So it is between your thoughts and your actions and your actions and your feelings.

Cognitive Behavioral Triangle

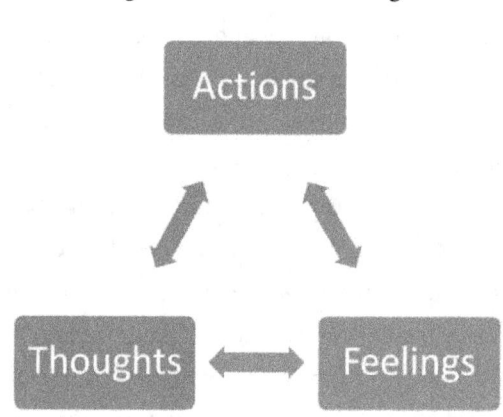

You don't have to be at the mercy of your feelings and thoughts. In fact, you have the response-ability to act in ways that will change your thoughts and feelings. You can choose to change your thoughts in ways that will affect your feelings and actions. It's difficult to feel differently on demand and change your actions and thoughts as a result, but you are most certainly not at the mercy of your feelings!

You can evaluate your feelings and how they tend to run you and decide if that's how you want to feel and if that's how you want to run. You can know thyself and examine your life. You have response-ability and that's why you have responsibility for the outcomes in your life. If you aren't happy with your outcomes, I've got great news for you. Ya ain't done yet!

*Real Talk Truth: You can change your behaviors, and with them your outcomes, to suit you. You've seen the sign, "Will Build to Suit." Well, you are the architect and builder of your life.*

*Whatcha Gonna Do? Take the time to write down what you suspect are the keystone habits that disrupt you from being your best you and building the life and business you desire. Then consider the thoughts and feelings that are influencing those habits.*

# Chapter 6
# It's Simple, but It Isn't Easy

*"People are disturbed not by events alone, but by the views that they take of them." –Epictetus*

Many of us think that events make us feel. We think events make us angry or sad or anxious. But that gives away your power. It's really about your view of the events. Would people think Andre Drummond looked funny shooting underhand in this day and age? I'm sure they would, but if his percentage went from 38% to 78% the joke is no longer him! Shooting 38% and having to sit out crunch time is the joke now. You can reframe the discussion in your mind to fit you. That's what Rick Barry's dad helped him to do with the statement, "they can't make fun of you if you make them." And why would anyone let outside events control their feelings and thoughts anyway? Your feelings and thoughts will greatly impact your actions and your actions control your outcomes—your destiny!

You need to understand the feelings and thoughts that are holding you back. You need to examine them and decide if those feelings and thoughts are going to support the actions you need to take to create your desired destiny or not.

Your core beliefs are controlling beliefs. If you believe deep down inside you that staring at someone is rude, you will be offended when people stare at you. I learned that when I lived in Eastern Europe and was stared at on the tram a lot. I was obviously American and the wall had just come down so Eastern Europeans were not used to seeing Americans on their public transportation. I got stared at a lot. I am from a place where staring at someone too long could cause them to get really mad. I was uncomfortable about being stared at. My deeply held (though not consciously examined) belief was triggering feelings which were leading to well-rehearsed thoughts. It didn't even occur to me that it wasn't rude initially. Fortunately, I had cultural insiders to talk to so I got over it.

The point is that our core beliefs are largely unexamined but are at work filtering all the possible feelings and thoughts that could happen and selecting only a few. Those core beliefs are controlling premises. If I start with the premise that the world should be fair, then when someone steals a parking spot from me I may feel outraged and have quick almost automatic thoughts about that. They are not really automatic per say, but they are so well rehearsed that they feel automatic. Your brain has so rehearsed these connections between those feelings of outrage (that are selected by your core beliefs) and those thoughts which may include that the parking spot thief deserves a finger salute. You may find yourself having the knee jerk chain reaction response of getting angry and almost automatically flippin' the bird. That is until you have children and they are in the back seat of your car every day. Then the core belief that modeling adult human behavior for your children is way more important than letting some jerk control your feelings, thoughts and actions like that may rewire your chain reaction. At least it should.

Please hear me when I tell you that these chain reactions of feelings, thoughts and actions are chains. They have us all bound up. They are the result of years and years of practice. They are well rehearsed, and you and I are on automatic with them. It takes very little effort for us to continue on the paths we are now on. These are comfortable and familiar. The question is, are these habits desirable? Make no mistake, they are habits and habits can be broken.

The point about rehearsal can't be overstated. Let me illustrate how automatic it becomes. The other day Tina and I took her sister and her sister's husband to the Detroit Tigers game. They live in New Zealand. He'd never been to America and had never seen a baseball game live. We got some bleacher seats in centerfield and a beverage or two. Tina and I were avoiding gluten so we got these frozen daiquiris in long plastic containers that make getting the last bit out of the bottom near impossible. It was between innings and the outfielders were tossing a ball around as they do. I was trying to dislodge that last bit of frozen drink at the bottom of my cup when suddenly everyone was standing up around me with excitement. Often the center fielder will toss the practice ball into the stands as a souvenir. I looked up and a baseball was flying out of the night sky, into the stands at me! Now I played a lot of sports in my life. Coached a lot of sports too so I have the well-rehearsed feeling , thought, action chain in me flowing from the core belief that I must catch a flying ball if I can reach it. So in a split second I rose to my feet, plucked it out of the air one handed to the loud snap sound of a baseball hitting flesh, stuck in my pocket, sat down and went straight back to the maddening activity of trying to get the last bit of my tasty treat. Those around me seemed impressed with the lack of effort that took. What they don't know is that it was the result of a tremendous amount of effort over years and years of rehearsing that exact activity (minus the daiquiri). Getting the last bit out of that ridiculous cup was not well rehearsed and was a clumsy activity to say the least.

So it is with all sorts of events that trigger feeling, thought, action chains in all of us all the time. You have years and years of rehearsal invested in your chains. They are knee jerk chain reactions as a result. They have you bound up in one way or another. That's ok if those chains of feelings, thoughts and actions are ones you're happy with, if they are ones you're proud of, if they are ones that lead to the outcomes you want in life. Because make no mistake about it, those chains will define and create your outcomes. Your destiny is bound up with those chains. Are your chains leading you to the life, the outcomes, the destiny you desire?

If you're honest with yourself, some of those chains have you bound up in a destiny you do not want. Some of those chains are chains you need to break free of. Some of those chains are holding you back. That's why this is called The Freedom Funnel. It is all about you breaking free of that which has held you back, held you down, held you away from your desired destiny!

I've got incredibly good news for you. Everyone knows you can change your mind, but you can even change your brain.

Habits are housed in a deep part of your brain known as the Basal Ganglia. It being deep in the brain lets us know it is a very old part of the human brain. It's fascinating because as we practice feelings, thoughts and behaviors and those chains become habits, the brain stores them deep in the Basal Ganglia and the synapsis required for those habits become hard wired and are like super highways in our brains. They happen with lightning efficiency. But they happen with very little effort at that point. They happen on automatic.

Habits acting on automatic with little effort for the brain are tremendously helpful if they are habits we are happy with. I've been driving cars for many years. It is really easy for me to do now. It requires almost no thought. I automatically know where the key goes, where the shifter, blinkers and pedals are. That's extremely helpful because without thinking about it I can operate a motor vehicle and my brain can still be engaged in other activities like carrying on a thoughtful conversation with a passenger or singing along with my favorite songs. That is until I found myself driving on a dark, and I mean dark, two lane highway on the wrong side of the car and the wrong side of the road in Fiji.

On our first trip to Fiji, we landed just before dusk and rented a car for the 60 minute drive to the resort. As I gassed up I met a young petrol station employee and asked him if we were on the right road to get where I wanted to go. In broken English he said it was and then said slowly while shaking his head slightly, "don't lost." "What?" I replied. Again he said, "don't lost." "Don't get lost you mean?" He said, as creepy as you could with a slow shake of the head while maintaining a chilling eye contact, "don't get lost." It sounded very much like the next sentence could have been, "they probably would never find the bodies." Ok, so that's obviously way too many scary movies talking, but it was creepy. So off into the darkness I drove. There were stray dogs popping up all of a sudden, people walking on the roads and wandering cattle. Yes, stray dogs, people and cattle popping up in the darkness!

Meanwhile, I'm not in my comfort zone of habit at all being that I'm sitting on the right side of the car and driving on the left side of the road. Every round about required I look to the right first. That was just weird. I spent my entire life looking left first. Left turns meant hugging the curve and right turns meant swinging out to the other side of the road. And who decided to put that damn blind spot on the right side of the car as I was trying to swing out across traffic lanes to make a right turn and end up on the left side of the road? Furthermore, judging the width of a car from the right side looking over to the left side as you swerve around pedestrians on a dark road is maddening!

I knew how to drive, but I had the well-rehearsed, super highway of synapsis, Basal Ganglia stored habits of driving in the USA. It was mentally exhausting to drive that hour in Fiji. But when I returned to the states, I got in my car and all of the habits of driving were alive and well. Thoughtlessly, I drove us home from my friend's house where we left our car. It was like riding a bike because our habits never actually go away.

Those super highway of synapsis, well-rehearsed habits are always there. We just have to invent and instill new ones to take the bypass in our brains. It's why bad habits are so hard to break. They are there forever waiting for us to open them back up and they are as strong as ever when we do. That's why alcoholics and gambling addicts and food addiction and everything else is a one day at a time reality. Have you ever tried to quit smoking?

Quitting smoking is easy, I did it a hundred times. I remember being a young man and balling up a soft pack, opening the window and throwing them out into the snow covered backyard. And then three hours later I was walking out into the snow to piece together broken cigarettes. It wasn't until I replaced the smoking with running a mile that I was eventually able to not quit quitting. The key is, and always will be, replacing the routine of the undesired habit with a routine of a new desired habit that also has a payoff when you get the cue to, in that case, smoke. The craving a smoke cue was followed by smoking and the satisfaction I felt was real. Even writing these words 30 years after the fact, I sense that I could pick up smoking pretty easily. But the trigger of craving got replaced with the running of a mile and that routine had a tremendous satisfaction that eventually replaced the urge to smoke and I didn't quit quitting anymore.

*Real Talk Truth: There are behavioral habits/routines in your life and business that need to be replaced by behavioral habits/routines that create your desired destiny.*

*Whatcha Gonna Do? As we progress in this book, you'll be given insight into what needs to be happening to create your freedom. Take an honest inventory of how you feel, what you think and whether or not your actions will create your desired outcomes as you go through The System section.*

# Chapter 7
# I've Got Good News

The good news is you have response-ability and can rewire your brain and create the thoughts, feelings, actions chain reactions that define the life you want and create the destiny you desire. You and you alone are responsible to make it happen, and it takes consistent work.

My father taught 30 years at the University of Michigan—Flint. He confided that by the time he retired he was pretty sick of Sociology 101. I only taught 12 years of Philosophy 101, but I could appreciate that he was looking forward to retirement and doing some of the things he always wanted to do. Unfortunately, it wasn't long after he retired that he suffered a massive stroke.

I was living in Minneapolis and working as a chaplain with the University of Minnesota Golden Gopher athletic department when I got the call that my dad was rushed to the hospital and to come quick if I wanted to see him before he died. Of course I got there as quickly as I could and he was pretty bad, but he made it through the initial crisis. I spent the next couple of years flying in as often as I could and then I moved the entire family back to Michigan to be near him. He died about 3 and half years after the stroke, but it wasn't from the stroke.

Before the stroke, his prostate was enlarged and the doctor told him they should keep an eye on it. When he was nearly killed by the stroke, they took their eye off it. When he was starting to get better from the stroke the doctor decided to check on that old prostate situation, but it was too late. The cancer had gotten into the bone and he died from it. He suffered greatly from wasting syndrome which is every bit as horrible as it sounds and more.

Through the years, before it got really bad, my dad worked to rewire his brain. The stroke had destroyed large parts of his brain and with it many functions of his body. But through hard, consistent work, he recovered much of the function he lost. If stroke victims can rewire their brains, you can.

My sister is a violinist. She graduated from the Interlochen Arts Academy, the Eastman Conservatory of Music and has two master's degrees: one in music theory and one in performance. She worked as a concert violinist for most of her adult life. She also suffered from epilepsy through all of that.

She contracted measles as a child. It is believed that the measles caused the epilepsy by damaging a part of her brain. Years later, as an adult in her late 30's and early 40's, she underwent several brain surgeries to cut out the part of her brain that was causing the electrical storms known as seizures. The medicine could no longer control them. She was forced to try a more radical approach.

One of the scariest parts of the surgery was that the portion of her brain to be removed is where music memory is normally housed. The old joke set up line of, "Doc, will I ever be able to play the violin again?" was a real concern for her. An entire lifetime of development may be lost and a lifetime of personal identity with it.

The neuro-surgeons were extremely interested to find out what was going to happen. The days following the surgeries were nail biters. The pictures of her in hospital gown and head bandaged with a violin under her chin and bow up are quite emotional to this day. The beauty of the human brain's ability to rewire is very real to my sister Martha. She played from memory a complicated Bach passage to the applause of doctors, nurses and staff!

The belief is that the portion of brain that should have been learning and housing music her whole life was damaged by the measles and subsequent epilepsy so her brain rewired around it. When they removed the damaged portion, the music was untouched. In no small way your choices create the brain's wiring. The behavior's you consistently engage in become the rehearsed pathways of your brain and become easier and easier to reproduce. The question is: are they the ones you desire?

You can create the brain you want by working on it wisely. You can create the thought, feeling, behavior chains that will build the freedom and life you envision for yourself. The Freedom Funnel System can show you how. The steps you need to take to build the business and life you want are simple, but the motivation is up to you. Do you want it? Are you willing to do what it takes to get it? Is your freedom important enough to you? If so, turn the page.

*Real Talk Truth: The feeling, thought, action chains (habits/routines) you need to have in order to create the outcomes you desire are within your reach. Because you have response-ability, you alone have responsibility to create your freedom.*

*Whatcha Gonna Do? It's up to you. The question isn't can you? The question is will you? Will you do what is required to create the business and with it the life you desire? You can. I'll help.*

# Chapter 8
# How Do You Know What's Important?

*"Happiness is an activity of soul in accordance with virtue."* —*Aristotle*

It all is important. That's the biggest challenge about real estate as a career. People who aren't professional realtors don't really understand that. They think what we do is easy. That's because we don't communicate everything we do. Part of that is because the real estate transaction in real time can be a bit like making sausage. It isn't always so pretty and not everyone has the stomach for it. Another part of it is because we don't really have a system that includes the communication with our people the way it should. It definitely isn't easy. I know what you go through to keep your business going. It can be a mammoth undertaking. I've been tempted to buy the t-shirt I've seen online that says, "I'm a real estate broker. I solve problems you didn't know you had in ways you couldn't understand." Isn't that the truth?

What you and I need to do to be successful is complex and varied. Because it's complex and varied, it is easy to get off track doing things that we think could be important, but in fact are not. Oh, they may be urgent, but getting pushed around by urgency leaves you wondering whether or not what you're doing is important. You need to *know* what you're doing is important. Hoping it is, is not a good way to do things. The key is to live a contemplative life.

## Contemplation Required

You ever wonder what the ancients were talking about when you read a quote like Aristotle's above? Me too, so I went to seminary and studied philosophy. Let me save you tens of thousands of dollars and a ridiculous number of hours in the library and tell you. This particular quote will change your life if you apply it.

It leads to the conclusion that the contemplative life is the happiest. It doesn't mean the sort of "happiness" that comes from your favorite ice cream. It's far deeper and more meaningful than that. Aristotle's word for it was *Eudamonia* and it has to do with a vital, fully realized existence. It has to do with an actualized potential. It has to do with thriving. A sort of thriving that comes from an intentional, some have said, purposeful way of living. And that starts with contemplation which is fancy for thinking it through.

The science that Madison Avenue (the center of the marketing industry) banks on tells us that we are more emotional than rational. These ancients understood it to be a function of our souls. They understood that we have a rational component, but we also have irrational components to our soul, i.e. appetites. This is the part of us that plies us off track and plies our money out of our pockets into the pockets of Madison Avenue's clients. How else do you explain the ludicrous behavior of a fast food nation? We knowingly give our hard earned money to strangers through (I refuse the thru spelling this industry has thrust upon us) a window and receive grease, salt and sugar through another window and call it a meal. Meals are meant to give nutrition not entertainment. They are meant to keep us strong and healthy not weak and eventually kill us.

So the key is to allow the rational component of our soul to primarily govern our existence. This does not mean we don't indulge our appetites for good food, good drink and good sex. We do it reasonably. And the third piece of cheesecake is never reasonable. In fact, I'm beginning to suspect the second piece wasn't either.

## Teleological Thinking

When Aristotle says thinking it through, he means all the way through to the end. Some call it "beginning with the end in mind". But that is still short of what can and probably ought to be done. Consider the very nature of human existence as a whole and yours in particular. We all share so many things in common. In an age that emphasizes individuality and diversity, we miss the remarkable similarities we share. Consider that we all have health and social needs that are amazingly alike. For instance, do you like money? Me too! Dude, we should hang out!

But seriously, we are way more similar than different in our genetic make-up and our socialization. The truth is, while we talk about diversity it is really more of an illusion in our increasingly homogenous culture. For instance, very few corporations control the bulk of what you consume. They just have different brands to give an appearance of choice. Proctor and Gamble, Monsanto and General Electric and the like own it somehow. That translates into our experiences of life being more similar than they once were when cultures and ethnic groups controlled more of their own worlds.

Contemplate the nature of human existence in general. We all have physical, intellectual, social, psychological, emotional and sexual needs. And when these categories are not sufficiently fulfilled our lives get out of balance. You know it when you see the workaholic ignoring the family or the emotionally needy person chasing off their best relationships. Aristotle called the balance "the golden mean" between extremes. For our purposes we can use this teleological thinking to contemplate what makes life good really? We can ask ourselves: am I spending my limited time and treasure in the direction that will make me happy?

Beyond the generalities that apply to all humans, we each have particular potential in a variety of areas. I played sport. I was even able to have my college tuition paid for through sport. I traveled to 20 nations on three different continents because of my involvement in sport. But if Michael Jordon had only ever realized the level of success in sport that I did, he would have been sorely disappointed, downright unhappy you could say. I was very happy with my level of success because I realized enough of my potential to get through University and see three continents of the world. Jordon had much more potential than that and realized it to the tune of an NCAA championship, an Olympic gold medal, 6 NBA championships and quite a lot of money in the process. I hope he also had sufficient realization of potential in the general categories of life so as to experience the balance that is necessary to be happy. It takes both the general and particular fulfillment to achieve happiness. Where are you winning and where are you losing in this quest to thrive?

I can't say I was doing very well. When I stopped and considered what was actually important to me, it was clear it was the kid's well-being that was the top of my list intellectually, but I was not winning. I had to make a decision to change my behaviors. I had to start acting on my core beliefs in ways that created the destiny I desired.

## Philosophical Wisdom

What we're talking about so far here is what Aristotle referred to as "philosophical wisdom." We've engaged in contemplating the sort of things that make life good really. To do this regularly is required. It is only a necessary part of thriving; it is not in itself sufficient. If you've ever thought about it for any length of time, you have come to the philosophical conclusion that good health is better than bad, that building wealth assets is better than debt and that a great relationship with a friend or family member is better than a bad one. Here we have knowledge, but it is power, if and only if, it is correctly applied.

There are more in depth parts to philosophical wisdom than these obvious surface conclusions and a lifestyle of contemplation will allow you to discover them. Some are very general like the ones above, but some are very specific to your existence. The most significant part of my existence is no longer sport as it was in my youth. I am father to five young people. They range from 18 to 26 as I write this and each one is their own individual. They share much in common but it would be a mistake to consider them all the same. Philosophical wisdom about each of them requires much contemplation. A contemplation that is not happening when the TV is on and Madison Avenue is bombarding my irrational components. It's not happening when Facebook is scrolling or Netflix is on either!

People are unique and what's important to them has to be taken into account. Even people from the same gene pool, raised by the same parents are different and contemplating them with all their uniqueness is required to reach philosophical wisdom about them. Take my sister the violinist for instance. She has a piano in her house.

It is a baby grand piano and takes up quite a bit of floor space. If someone took it away, it would greatly impact her happiness in a negative way. I had a piano for a long time that no one ever played. With five kids and a large dog in the house it added to my happiness when it went away (hopefully to someone who loved having it) because it added space to my family's crowded existence at the time.

## Practical Wisdom

It's not enough to think about what generally makes life good or even what specifically makes life good for you and yours. We must move from philosophical wisdom to practical wisdom. The next question is: what will you do about it? Contemplate what you should do about this philosophical wisdom you now have. If acquiring wealth is better than laboring under debt, do you think budgeting and making sure you spend less than you make is a good idea? Do you think that cash flow in your life should be used to build future wealth through investment rather than just put in your mattress? Do you think it's important to have the right sort of insurance to prevent some future event from taking away all the wealth you accumulate over time?

Well of course the answer to all of these questions is yes. They are easy questions. Then why do so many of us live above our means and find ourselves overwhelmed by debt? Why do we spend our money first on housing we can't afford, transportation we can't afford and even entertainment we can't afford and then hope there will magically be some left over for our future somehow? Aristotle would tell us it is because we are not primarily governed by our rational components and are not applying the philosophical wisdom that contemplation can bring.

We are being played like a tune by a relatively few Madison Avenue elites that bombard our irrational components daily. We are not exercising our liberty to define our existence for ourselves and build our American Dream of a debt free life in a paid for house and able to retire at a reasonable age. We are in fact allowing our existence to line the pockets of the wealthy investor class by allowing ourselves to be turned from citizens to consumers and that robs us of happiness. We become expendable workers and consumers that labor all week to get enough money to meet our obligations and spend a little extra on trivial items that don't satisfy. We spend our lives on the treadmill that the wealthy profit from.

We must take the philosophical wisdom contemplation brings and go right back to thinking. We must consider what we should be doing about it. We must make plans and goals. We budget, invest and continue to think about what's best for our existence and happiness. With our families we must invest our time in ways that demonstrate love to them. We all know the golden rule of doing unto others as we would have them do unto us. But it still requires contemplation because part of doing unto others as we would have them do unto us is to consider what would be a blessing to them. We wouldn't want anyone to buy a gift for us based on their preferences. We want them to consider who we are and buy us a gift that we would like. We can't treat our children like we want to be treated. We have to consider who they are and treat them accordingly. After all, that is how we would have others do unto us.

Practical wisdom takes the philosophical wisdom and builds an action plan around it. Whether it is wealth management, parenting, our real estate businesses or any other area of life we need to contemplate the best courses of action for us as individuals and act accordingly.

Here I want to pause on Aristotle's philosophy long enough to insert some practical wisdom. When it comes to our plans, we must make goals. But we must make two very different sort of goals to ultimately succeed. We must make Stretch Goals and SMART Goals.

You've probably heard of SMART Goals somewhere along the line and Stretch Goals are no stretch to understand. But they are both vital to your Freedom! We'll return to the importance of each type of goal at the end of this chapter. Now we rejoin our regularly scheduled programming and return to Aristotle's *eudemonia*. To recap, we were talking of philosophical wisdom (the insight contemplation brings to what makes life good in general and particularly for you) and practical wisdom (the thoughtful planning regarding what you should do about the insights gained through philosophical planning).

## Moral Virtue

Even if we contemplate what makes life good long enough to gain some philosophical wisdom, and even if we think about what we should do about it long enough to gain some practical wisdom, we still have not done what it takes to reach our dreams and desired outcomes. We must also, Aristotle tells us, have "moral virtue." This refers to the habits that make life good really. When it comes to our money, it's not enough to look at the wisdom of building wealth and the freedom that brings to our existence. It's not enough to make the plan that will allow us to realize our dream of financial freedom. It requires the moral virtue, the habitual behaviors, that actually allow us to realize our potential. Make no mistake, your outcomes are a function of the habits you have. You cannot contemplate your way to freedom. You must behave your way to freedom.

The whole process is what brings about happiness. It is the process of hard work and the incremental progress it brings. For instance, the incremental progress toward the eventual achievement of giving the final investment check on your mortgage that makes your home free and clear of any encumbrance that makes us happy.

For Aristotle, happiness is an activity of soul (reasoning) in accordance with virtue (reasoning well). Because it is this contemplation that will give you the philosophical wisdom to know what makes your existence good and the practical wisdom to know what to do about it. Both of these are necessary but not sufficient for your thriving and happiness because knowledge is power, if and only if, it is correctly applied. Happiness (*eudemonia*) requires the moral virtue to habitually behave in the way that fulfills your American Dream of financial freedom. For as Rousseau said, "The money we possess is the instrument of liberty. The money we do not possess, but seek to obtain, is the instrument of slavery." You can do it. Babe Ruth said, "a person who never gives up is hard to defeat."

Babe Ruth's point is a powerful concept. Talent is not the number one factor in success. In my years as a sports chaplain I ventured into many prisons and juvenile detention centers with world class athletes. I assure you there is more talent behind bars than there is in all of our professional sports leagues combined. No, talent is not the key. Grit is the key. Old fashioned nitty gritty, never give up, see it through and figure it out grit. But you must see the right things through. Sticking to a losing game plan is foolish.

# Section 2

# The System

# Chapter 9
# Win With Your Strengths; Don't Let Your Weaknesses Beat You

The Freedom Funnel recognizes that the tasks of the real estate professional are complex and varied. In order to have a viable business you have to do all of them well. In order to have a great business you have to do them with excellence. Greatness comes from doing the basics with excellence over and over. But no one is good at everything.

At the end of the 2015-2016 season, Tim Duncan retired from professional basketball after 19 seasons in the NBA. He played until he was 40 years old! Duncan was the first pick of the 1997 draft, won five NBA Championships, was league MVP twice, was named an All-Star 15 times and is the only player to be an All-Star and named to the All Defense team for each of his first 13 seasons.

I bring him up because of his nickname. Players get nicknames because of their game. Famously, Earvin Johnson from Lansing, Michigan was known as "Magic" because of the tricks he pulled off during the game. Tim Duncan was all business and not the least bit tricky. Nonetheless, he's widely regarded as the greatest power forward in history. All of his success came directly from the trait his nickname illustrates. Tim was known as "The Big Fundamental."

He, maybe more than anyone he played with or against is the shining example of the power of doing the little things with excellence over and over and how that leads to greatness. But that said, Duncan was asked to do only so much. Being a 7-footer, he was not asked to dribble the ball up court. He was not asked to defend the quickest guards on the other team. He certainly was not asked to take care of the equipment, manage the players, make personnel decisions, make travel plans or arrange financing for the arena. In fact it would be absurd to ask the starting power forward to do anything other than the power forward's job. The key was to get good at the right things and not to worry about anything else.

Another excellent example of practicing the right things and it paying off is found in David Bayles and Ted Orland's book *Art and Fear*. They tell the story of the ceramics teacher that experimented on his class by telling half of them that they were being graded on quality and the other half they were being graded on quantity. In fact the quantity half were told that to get an A grade they had to use up 50 pounds of clay making pots! While the quality group was paralyzed by perfectionism the quantity group got busy practicing the behavior that allowed them to move toward mastery. In the end, all of the best quality pots came from the quantity group.

You already know this though. You heard the old joke about the NYC cab driver that was asked by his fare, "how do you get to Carnegie Hall?" "Practice, practice, practice" says the cabbie. Unfortunately, the real estate business is not as narrow as making the same pot over and over until you get good at it. What are the keystone habits that make a real estate business great? What are the behaviors that will lead to your freedom? I'm glad you asked because it is vital that the grit is correctly applied.

The problem with real estate is that the activities we have to do are remarkably varied and complex. In fact, we do have to make it all happen ourselves. From soup to nuts, it's on us. Take a look at the variety of segments represented on the following infographic. It helps to get a simplistic bird's eye view so you can see that it is not as overwhelming as it feels when you're in the weeds trying to make it all happen at once.

The Freedom Funnel (Overview)

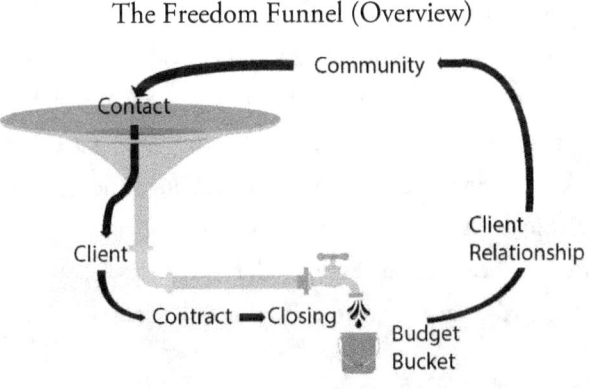

Take it from the top. To have a business that creates freedom for you, you need to turn your community into your contacts, your contacts into your clients, your clients into contracts and contracts into closings because that's where the cash is. But you're not done there because post-closing you need a continued client relationship that leads you deeper into your community, i.e. referrals!

The key to freedom is to work effectively in each of these segments. If you drop the ball at any point, you will not build a business that creates the future you envision. You will not reach your desired destiny. The answer is to create systems within each segment and make sure you work effectively within each system consistently. You must not neglect or half step your way in any of these.

You have to do all of these simultaneously and each segment around the loop involves a completely different set of skills. Turning community into contacts is a complex and varied set of skills and turning those contacts into clients is an entirely different skill set all together. Putting clients into contracts is yet another set of skills and so on and so on.

To compound the problem, no one, and I mean no one, is great at all of these things. We all have strengths and weaknesses. Denying that fact will only end up biting you in the butt later. Some of us have fragile enough egos that we have to tell ourselves we don't have weaknesses. We think we are in fact good at everything. You are not. As an attempt to make ourselves feel better we have taken to saying things like strengths and "needs to be developed." If that helps, go with that. But for goodness sake, face the truth. The truth shall set you free!

If you do not know thyself as well as Socrates would like, you can find all sorts of personality assessments. A very popular one is the Meyers-Briggs. It helps people know what their more natural and comfortable types of situations and behaviors are. It also lets people know what is less natural and less comfortable. Those are the activities and situations that will likely trip you up. At any rate, it is a great idea to have a strong sense of who you naturally are and who you are not!

When you know what your shortcomings are, you can address them. If you are great at winning people over and driving the business in the first place, but not so great at the careful and consistent communication as the process continues, it will beat you. You will disappoint people in the end and not get the great references and referrals that build your business. Then you'll compensate for that by going back to what you're good at and go find more people to win over so you have continued business. You'll be chasing business your entire career instead of building a business. You'll be good at it and that will reinforce your behavior. But you will only ever have a job that requires your presence. You will never build a business that enables your freedom!

I know this particular version of letting the weakness beat you intimately. But there are other versions. Versions that end up washing people out entirely. The point is to build up your weaknesses so they don't beat you or limit you. Work on your strengths so they are winners for you, AND work on your weaknesses so they are NOT losers for you.

Both parts of the last sentence are important. We've focused on not letting your weaknesses beat you, but it's also important to focus on winning with your strengths. If you're playing tennis and you have a big forehand, hit it like you mean it! If you have a so-so backhand, make sure you put it in play deep and look for the forehand. Don't try to hit winners with the backhand. When a player figures out how they win matches, it's a combination of winning with their strengths and not letting their weaknesses beat them. A light goes on in their head: Bingo! Yahtzee! We have a winner! That's exactly right. Win with your strengths.

Watch the end of an NBA game. When it's winning time, the ball goes to their best player. The NBA finals of 2016 were a great example. The Golden State Warriors, led by their star player Steph Curry, versus the Cleveland Cavaliers led by Lebron James. The Warriors set a record by winning 73 out of 82 regular season games. They only lost 9 games all season! They led the best of seven series 3 games to 1. But when it was time to win, James out played Curry. The ball went to James and the Cavaliers were able to win with their strengths.

What are you good at? When it comes to our strengths, we generally are in our natural comfort zones and are operating intuitively. We're just doing what we do without thinking about it. I once taught a University level class in the Philosophy of Leadership. In preparation I spoke with an author on leadership who confided in me that there are two kinds of leaders: one that leads intuitively and one that leads systematically. He said the best are intuitive. The problem with them is that you can't transfer their intuitions. The systematic leadership style can be transferable because you can share the system.

That thought has stayed with me. Applying it here, we can see that the complex and varied skill sets that are required to have a great real estate business are sometimes in your natural and intuitive wheelhouse and sometimes are in a not so natural zone which requires the transfer of a system to support you. That's what we have here. A system that can strengthen your strengths so you win, AND a system that can strengthen your weakness so you don't lose.

*Real Talk Truth: No one is good at everything and the weakest link in your business can cause you to never build a business that leads to freedom. You will forever only have a job.*

*Whatcha Gonna Do? Take a good long look at The Freedom Funnel infographic and ask yourself where you are winning and where you are losing. Are you working with bad leads because you don't have enough to choose from? Are you getting sufficient referrals from your past clients? If not where did your performance break down to prevent it from happening? Take the time to question and identify where you are really. Write it down.*

# Chapter 10
# Community to Contact:
# Top of Funnel Activity

The Freedom Funnel has three distinct levels: Top, Middle and Bottom. It is vital to focus on top of funnel activities and to recognize they are not real estate related activities. I repeat, not real estate related activities. The top of funnel is about connecting with your community. It is about being in touch with people way before real estate matters have entered their brain. What do you have to offer your community besides real estate services? Don't get it twisted, you will be a real estate expert that is offering these things, but it is not real estate expertise you are offering at this point. Your job is to turn your community into your contacts at this point.

Community to Contact (Top of Funnel)

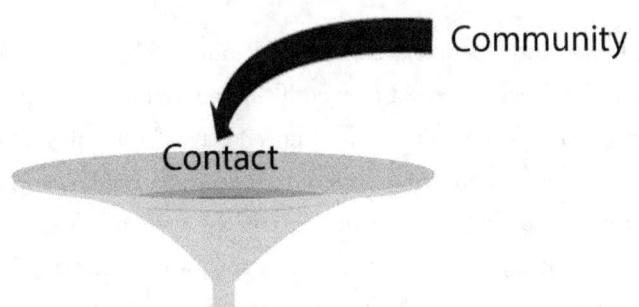

Does that sound counter intuitive to you? Does it sound like the wrong move entirely? Maybe it seems absurd to spend time and effort being known in your community for something other than real estate. Here's why: people do business with those they know, like and trust. If you wait until they have need for your real estate expertise to try to create relationship with them, you at best will only ever have a transactional relationship with them. A transactional relationship is a one and done relationship. And then you will be spending time and marketing dollars looking for another one and done transactional relationship.

If you create good will and relationship before they need real estate services, you will get their friendship. With their friendship, you will get their business when they have need of your expertise, AND you will get their referrals before and after they need your help personally.

People love to have a guy. In fact, I'm known by my friends and family for that phrase, "I gotta a guy." It feels really good to be able to refer people that I know, like and trust to other people that I know, like and trust. Because I "gotta guy" (many of whom are gals), people ask me when they need something. It ranges from where to get your car fixed to where to get your hair done (and I'm bald).

More importantly, people are up to 70% more likely to use a service that they have been referred to even if that referral is an anonymous online referral. You've done it; I know I have. You pull out your phone and look at an online referral service like YELP before you decide where to eat. Or even better, you ask a friend or two their opinion about a good place to go for a special birthday dinner. In fact, tonight we're headed to a place that a friend recommended for a special dinner.

If you're a person that has been honestly helpful to people in a variety of ways at the top of your funnel, you will enjoy the fruits of that when their friends and family are in need of real estate services. That is, if you do it right.

Doing it right means offering something that others want and need besides your real estate services. It means being a valuable part of your community. An easy way to see this for many is through their church participation. Two of my most productive agents over the years are an important part of their local churches. One is the organist and helps out with all of the music. She brings who she is and what she has to offer her community to church week after week and has earned their respect. The other is a youth leader and organizes the church's softball team. He loves young people and sports. That is who he is and what he has to offer his community.

Neither of them do it to get business. They do it because that's who they are. But they are not secret agents either. They purposely work the fact they are real estate agents into their daily conversations. It's not hard to do. It's just talking about your day. Not complaining about your day ever! Always positive. Things like, "this young couple I'm helping find their first home are so cute." Or, "I saw a really great kitchen when I was showing houses this week. I was so jealous." Neither sentence is about being a real estate agent, but they both remind the listener that you are a real estate agent!

You have interests that would make your life better to participate in more fully. I had an agent that plays tennis. He gets business from his team and the teams he competes against at the local tennis clubs. I have another agent that loves live theater but could never see himself on stage. He can however help out with set building and does. The theater community in our area is huge!

I spent years and years coaching kids in the park. I coached until my kids were too old to participate anymore and now I sit on the board of the non-profit that runs the leagues. It's my job to help them land sponsors for the teams. So I volunteer and mingle with business owners in my community. Do you think business owners ever know anyone looking for a local expert in real estate?

Again, it's not to get business. I volunteer because I want to be a real and valued part of my community. But it pays off as I go. I know business owners all over town. When people I know need something, I gotta a guy. When I refer the people in my community business, they like me. When they know, like and trust me, guess who gets their referrals for real estate?

But how do we take it up a notch? How do we get a wider profile than the personal involvement we can create through volunteering? Don't let what I'm about to tell you stop you from volunteering and being involved. There are at least two reasons why it is absolutely vital to stay personally involved in your community at a grass roots level. One is because it will make your life significantly better. Humans are wired through evolution to be part of a tribe and to have something to offer their people. As you give, you will thrive in life. It is truly more blessed to give than to receive. The second reason is because of authenticity. Those of us who try to give from 30,000 feet and not from the ground level are not thought of as real folks. We are thought of as hypocrites looking for photo ops. Sorry, right or wrong, it's true. Stay involved at a grass roots level with the things that matter to you.

You really can do so much more for your business than the old school approach we've been talking about. You can amplify it through media and social media. I learned this through the radio show we started years ago. That's where Michigan Real Talk started. It started with the notion that using media can and does set you apart from the crowd. Picking up the phone and calling with the introduction, "Hi, this is Paul Curtis, host of Michigan Real Talk" opened doors to relationships we never would have had. I know most of you reading this are thinking, "there is no way I could do that." It's not for everyone for at least two reasons: one, because it is a lot of work, and two, because it doesn't fall into the natural comfort zones of many people. It would be the equivalent of trying to win with your weakness. It's foolish to even consider for most. But for some it is a really good idea.

I moved from radio to TV and the step was huge. It wasn't just a little different. It was a lot different. It stretched me out of my comfort zone, but it still was in the realm of strength and a win for me. It just took some work. But maybe radio and TV are not the media for you. Possibly writing books could work. Certainly writing a blog could work. Blogs are short and don't require significant research like books do. But they do require consistency.

At any rate, you can and should distinguish yourself from the crowd by using media. Here though you have to be operating as a real estate expert. In the prior discussion about being connected to your community in a meaningful way, it was about authenticity as a member of the community and a source for meaningful relationships. When it comes to the use of media, it is about showing yourself to be an authority in real estate. A blog about politics won't do it. Writing (books and blogs) or talking (radio and television) about the American Dream of homeownership and real estate investment will position you above the others in your market. Imagine the lead that is interested in selling and you send them your top three blog articles on their market and how they can maximize their sale. Or imagine sending them the youtube clip of your television show where you're the star explaining how to get top dollar in their market. That's not an email many will be able to send.

Not only does it set you apart with leads, it sets you apart with leaders. Of course we want to reel in the contacts we make, and your use of media will help do that. But more importantly, you will be able to open doors with leaders you would have been just another real estate agent to before. There is nothing more valuable in business than relationships. Setting yourself above the crowd as the authority in your market and using media to promote others is a relationship building activity. Relationships mean referrals if you develop them correctly. And media helps you fast track the relationships you are looking for.

Now imagine you are interested in getting to know business and political leaders in your area and you have a radio show. Calling up and saying, "this is Paul Curtis, host of Michigan Real Talk, and we're doing an upcoming segment on _____ (fill in the blank with their expertise). Would you have something to say on that subject?" Well of course they do. And they would love the platform to say it. Now you've gotten the chance to meet them. Set a pre interview appointment at their office. You meet the key people on their staff. You prepare a set of questions with their assistance that will allow them to hit the subject out of the park on your show. Take them to lunch following the show. Take a photo of them in studio with you and have it framed as a follow up gift. Send them the clip of their appearance as a file they can use after the airing to send to their database which shows them to be the sought after expert in their area. Before the show airs, create a promo card with their picture and logo so they can promote their appearance on your show. You now have been introduced to their sphere as an expert in your field and they have used your status to promote themselves to their people as an expert in their field.

Are you seeing what I'm talking about? Media can fast track relationship. Furthermore, it fast tracks the relationships you want in your sphere. I work in a market where one particular agent has spent decades building relationship through his involvement in the local chamber of commerce and city government. When he saw me sitting with the mayor drinking beer at a chamber after hours event he made a bee line to our table. The mayor asked if we knew each other. I said, "yes, of course we do." He said, "yes, the enemy." I got to take the high road and say, "now, now there is plenty of business for everyone" in front of the mayor. It was funny though, because I had just met the mayor a few weeks earlier and he had spent decades building a relationship with him. That same agent had a tag line at local events. When he introduced himself he would state his name followed by, "realtor to the stars." I introduced myself following him at one of those events as "Paul Curtis, star realtor!" I think you see what I'm talking about by now.

I want to repeat though that you should not try to do this at 30,000 feet. You need to be involved at a grassroots level too. There is real power in authentic involvement on the ground. If you try to skip that, you run the risk of looking like some media using carpet bagger that no one really likes. But the one who is doing both, that one is golden.

But what if radio isn't for me you ask? What if I'm camera shy? If by camera shy you mean TV, well ok. I'll let you off the hook. If by camera shy you mean pics on the web, get over yourself right now! Floyd Wickman is a longtime coach for real estate agents based out of Detroit. He tells the story of the agent who wouldn't even put his photo on his business card. Floyd asked him why not? The agent said that he was too ugly. As only Floyd could, he responded, "they're going to find out sooner or later. What, are you just going to show up and surprise them?" Floyd cracks me up.

You are going to have to put yourself out there. You are going to have to get past yourself and be your "best you" out there. There are too many run of the mill agents in the world already. Be extraordinary. Bring all of you to the table and bring your community what they want.

If it's a blog, don't just write about the housing market. Write about the wider market. That is, write about what makes your market so wonderful. Is it the walkable downtown and night life? Is it the amazing schools and their extracurricular activities? Is it the great programs for youth? Is it the arts? If you're in a community like mine, it is all of the above and more. It's a target rich environment for subject matter. Make sure you always bring it back to why that makes the housing market so incredible though. Never allow the reader/audience to lose track of the fact that you are a real estate authority and expert. When it comes to media, you are the go to real estate expert in your market that is bringing the community the extra benefit of showing it off right down to places to eat and drink and enjoy.

## Community You've Met

You need to stay in front of the community you've met without annoying them. Grow your social media presence not just your media usage. If you have a media presence, you also have social media content! After this writing session today, I'm headed to the TV studio to look at this week's show in order to identify segments we can edit into snippets we'll use in social media posts. These snippets will include sections that make our guests look great so they'll use them in their social media posts. That way I'll be in front of my already met community as the "go to expert" in my market, AND I'll be in front of their "already met community" which expands my "haven't met yet community" in the process.

But if your entire social media presence is about you, people will tune you out in a hurry. Let your content be about the world you share with your community. Let it be about your life with them. Just yesterday, there was a bomb threat at a downtown business in my town by someone claiming to be associated with a terrorist group. The businesses there were evacuated. Local police, state police, the FBI, etc. were involved. Ultimately the bomb sniffing K9s were called in and the scene was cleared. It was concluded that it was not a credible threat. Well, today I'm going to those businesses to buy something and posting on social media that we need to have each other's back in our town.

That's a heavy example. I also posted a short video of kids and their pets Monday morning that had to make someone smile. We post about the local high school sports teams, local night life, local politics, and so on. I know I mentioned the "P" word—politics. You can choose to ignore it and pretend it isn't there because you think avoiding it is good for your business. For years I did that. Recently, I decided I would be better off in my life to let people know who I am and let the chips fall where they may. I'm sure some people have faded in regards to liking me. But I'm equally sure others have strengthened in their respect for me. I won't tell you what to do with this one, but I will say that being yourself is important.

When I say, being yourself is important, I mean being your best self is important. Seems like nowadays you have to clarify sometimes. Authenticity is vital, but if you're authentically a mess, maybe you should think about becoming a better you. Let your social media posts be thought of as job interviews in that regard. Not that you have to talk about you and your job skills all the time, but rather be on your best behavior. No one goes to a job interview drunk for instance. Don't drink and post either if you catch my drift. Be positive about the world. There's a quote from Paul of Tarsus I've always loved: "Do everything without complaining or arguing so that you... shine like stars in the world." You want to stick out in this world? Be positive and upbeat. Everyone around you is negative. You'll shine like a star in the darkness.

Part of being your best you is exuding your mission and values. Do you have a clear understanding of those? Do you have a 30 second elevator version? Do you have a three minute testimonial version? If someone asked you to keynote an event and speak on your mission and values as it relates to your real estate business, do you know what you would say? My guess is most of you can't say yes to all three of those questions. You should be able to though.

I don't quote Popes often, but when I do I quote John Paul II when he said, "profit is not sufficient motivation for business." I believe what he meant by that was that if you're only in it for money, if you don't have a bigger why than that, then you are not really doing anything worth doing. Please understand that profit is a necessary motivation for business, but it's not a sufficient one. Necessary but not sufficient is a logic term that is easily understood by the example of ice. Water is necessary for ice but not sufficient. You also need a temperature below 32 degrees to get ice. Profit is necessary for business. Without it, the business can't last long and whatever good it can do for others will cease. But profit is not enough. You need a Big Why in your business. What is your Big Why and can you communicate it in a compelling way?

You should take a break from reading and write down some of your thoughts. Don't put it off. Do it now. Answer these three questions as a start:

1. Why do we do what we do?
2. What does success look like?
3. How must we act to ensure success?

I'm including my vision for my team here for you to see what it looks like. But you need to write out your vision so you can be true to yourself. Here's mine. It led to this book.

> *"Humanity yearns for freedom. Rousseau (1712-1778) said, 'The money we possess is the instrument of freedom. The money we do not possess, and seek to obtain, is the instrument of slavery.' The bumper sticker says, 'I owe, I owe so off to work I go.' When we bring our clients to the right home ownership situation for them, we bring them a step closer to freedom because home ownership is a foothold to a future financial freedom. And there is no freedom without financial freedom.*
>
> *Furthermore, humans have evolved from tribal environments. We are all the product of some people and some place. There is nothing more human than having a place to belong to and a people to be there with. Besides the obvious financial benefits of home ownership, we are helping our clients find their place to be in community.*

*For our agents, we must help them find their path to freedom. Training them to attract and retain referral generating clients is not enough. It is not how much you make in this business but how much you keep that matters. The agent that is working from passion rather than compulsion is the agent we want. If our agents are moving down their path to freedom successfully, they can passionately help others as well. Our agents should be helping others find their path to freedom because they want to, not because they have to find another closing this month or next.*

*This requires us to be early adapters of technology and experts in our markets. We must distinguish ourselves as not just players on our client's (and agent's) Dream Team of experts, but as captains of that team. We must be the center of our referral networks. We must have a network of experts from mortgages to retirement planning, from car repair to hair care and beyond. Our clients must know we are the go to person in their sphere for local referrals in everything they need. We do this through the use of media: local podcasts, local TV talk shows, and local social media networking. We will be at the center of it as the Realtors of choice.*

*And so we seek to help all (clients and agents) own their American Dream as in take personal responsibility for it so they can own their American Dream as in achieve it. We help others reach the American Dream of a debt free life in a paid for house and able to retire at a reasonable age for freedom's sake. So many Americans find themselves in survival mode. We, as a nation, are running to our second job and dropping bad carry out food on the table for our children. We must move from survive to thrive so that we can have an impact. The world needs us. Our communities need us to coach the kids in the park, tutor the kids at the schools, and run for local governments to better serve our neighbors. We must succeed at bringing freedom to ourselves and our clients so we may be the difference we long to see in the world."*

Those are my words. You need to find yours. Take the time now to begin writing it out. Answer the three questions above as a starting point. Your vision can't be a secret. If you want to make contacts in your community, let your community know your vision. Have a 30 second version, a three minute version, and one day, have a 30 minute version. Be able to deliver those versions with passion. You'll find the passion you have for your vision will sustain you in the daily grind of business and attract others to you.

The 30 second version will be extremely valuable in the networking opportunities you find yourself in. Truth be told, I hated networking meetings. Rooms full of people with business cards in their pockets looking for opportunities to give them to each other. Nothing was less fun for me. One because I hate going around with my hand out trying to get people to like me and two because I hate it when people do that with me. But I love my passion for freedom. When I can be in networking situations now, I treat them like parties. I find people to talk to about things other than my business and ask them questions about themselves. The clueless ones answer the questions and hand me a business card. The thoughtful, interesting people talk to me like a real person and we get the chance to talk about what's really important to us as people. It's a lot of fun to hear from them and to share with them my passion for freedom. Often they end up asking me what I do for work and I get to tell them a little about our real estate business. But more importantly, I get to make friends and develop relationships around my vision and passion for furthering freedom in the world.

The reason you need to start by writing it out is so that you're well versed, rehearsed and thoughtful when you have the chance to talk about it. Passion is communicated through fluidity not stammering. You've got to have a flow for your vision and a rhythm to your communication. You need to be able to turn a phrase if you want to attract people and business.

Someone reading this is thinking that flow comes from not over thinking it and sitting down to write it out is the wrong way to achieve flow. Let me share something a very prominent public speaker once told me. He had traveled to over 170 nations as a presenter at the time he told me this. He said, if you want me to speak for 30 minutes, just give me five minutes to prepare. If you want 15 minutes, I'll need a couple of hours. If you want five minutes, give me a week. I'm telling you to have it down to 30 seconds. 30 seconds of impact regarding your passion and vision. Take it seriously and work on it. It will make a huge difference in how your life goes. When you know your vision and your passion well enough to articulate it meaningfully in just 30 seconds, you know yourself. And as Socrates said, that is the key to living well. "Know Thyself." I'm telling you the simplicity on the far side of complexity is worth the time it takes to hone that vision and message. When you have it down and mean it, you have a power to connect with people that will help you enormously.

Finally, when it comes to Community to Contact, you have to realize that in the 21st century you are first a website before you are a person.

Of course that's not literally true, but you should figure it is. People will search you before they'll talk to you these days. Your internet presence matters. Your website matters supremely. It doesn't have to be the most expensive website, but it can't suck. The same principles apply. If it's a strength of yours, then you need to win with it. If it is a weakness, you need to make sure it doesn't beat you. You need it to keep you in the game until you can work things around to your strengths.

In case you don't believe me about the importance of your website, check this out. A recent study from the National Association of Realtors discovered that the median age of first time buyers was 31. First time buyers that were married couples and first time buyers that were single men were also a median age of 31. The median was 32 for first time buyers that were single women. If the first time buyers were unmarried couples, the median age dropped to 28. Where are millennials looking all day every day? At their handheld screens! How do you look in there? I've said it over and over, put the fact that they're all staring at their phones all day with the culture's craving for immediate gratification and I don't care how many beers you bought your buddies. Whoever is in that screen when they start thinking about buying or selling is going to have the mind share necessary to get the business. If your website and web presence are on point, you win. If not, you lose.

So let's talk some minimums as it relates to your real estate website.

1.  Mobile ready or bust. Make sure you're on a platform that works on their fancy phones. If you're not a quick, and I mean quick click to looking good in the palm of their hand than you are not in the game.

2. Full IDX search that looks good and has mapping features. Now two things matter here. One is that you will not displace Zillow, Trulia, Realtor.com or the likes so don't try. You don't need an expensive app for that. However, number two is that as cool as you think you are, they want houses not you. And if you don't give them what they want, you lose. At this stage of the game, IDX is as much defense as it is offense. Not having it makes you look bad more than having it makes you look good. Sorry, just sayin'.

3. You need a clear and uncluttered layout. I can't over state this. Too many sites have too much going on. Go with the less is more approach as it relates to your layout. One way to accomplish this is to use calls to action a lot. Instead of embedding all the information, give them some add like content that asks them to "click here for more." Getting clicks on your pages is a win.

4. Make sure they are clicking to fresh and helpful content. Keep in mind that you are still high up in the funnel. It may be middle of the funnel, but it's upper middle. They are looking for great useful content. Give it to them. Give it to them for free. Don't play coy and put it behind gates that require they give you their contact information to get what they are looking for. That said, always and I mean always, have the opportunity to contact you just a click away. Forms matter. Make them available to fill out when they have a question. That's your chance to move them to the bottom of the funnel!

5. Use video content everywhere. People want to watch their internet more than they want to read it these days. But don't use autoplay features. You don't want to out them at work or church or where ever they are looking at their phones when they should be doing something else.

6. Give away your best. I'll say it again, give away your best. Make them like you through your content and make them think there's more where that came from. That's how you win!

There's much more to say about websites, but this is good enough for now. There are plenty of services out there for real estate specific websites, or you can get professional help building your own if that's important to you. One advantage to building your own is that you own it and don't have on going fees associated with it. But you also don't have behind the scenes people working on it. As I said, there is much more to say about websites, but that's enough for now.

This section wouldn't be complete without a word about paid services for leads. Mostly the answer is — you don't need them. Zillow has figured out how to take our listing information and use it to generate leads in our markets so they can sell them to us. They're not the only ones. Realtor.com and others promise to get us leads that we can turn into deals. They are mostly transactional relationships at best and cost us money to get them.

If you'll do what The Freedom Funnel says, you won't need the paid for services. That said, I know lots of agents use them. I've used them. I've closed some business through them. The biggest problem with them (besides they cost you money) is that you can get dependent on them and not do what you need to do to achieve freedom. If you think you can honestly ween yourself off them as you apply these principles, then go ahead. But most won't. Not that you can't, but it's likely you won't. That's for you and the man (or woman) in the mirror to work out.

*Real Talk Truth: The combination of authentic grassroots involvement in your community AND the amplification of media are a powerful combination to turn your community into contacts. But you must engage your community before they have need of real estate expertise AND you must do it as a real estate expert. Don't be a secret agent.*

*Whatcha Gonna Do? Ask yourself what the highest and best involvement in your community is for you. Should you run for office in local government because you always wanted to? Should you get involved at your kids school somehow? Who are you and if you could, how would you like to engage your community? Figure out a plan and do it, AND figure out how to amplify your presence through media. More later.*

# Chapter 11
# Contact to Client

Now we're in the Middle of the Funnel. You've positioned yourself as the go to person in your market and people want to talk to you when they have questions. If you've done your job at the Top of the Funnel well, getting people from the Middle to the Bottom is a piece of cake. The only real issues have to do with your capacity and organization to work with people.

Contact to Client (Middle of Funnel)

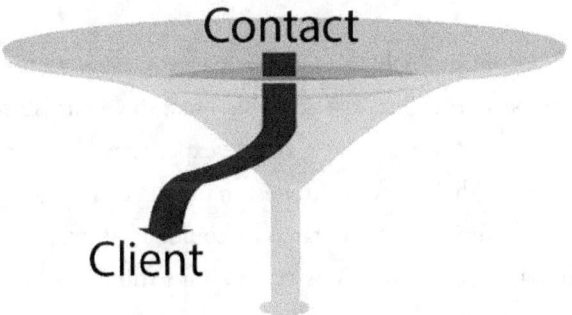

It may be you are operating out of a natural strength here in the middle of the funnel. It may be that communication and organization are like second nature to you. You may be extremely good at time blocking and communicating systematically so that everyone you have contact with regarding real estate matters feels as though they have your upmost attention. But, whether or not that's your strong suit, you need the right CRM working for you. A CRM is a Contact Relationship Manager. And it is worth its weight in gold.

You are probably, if you're a real estate agent, good with face to face and chit chat. You are probably fairly outgoing and can attract people. But the outgoing extrovert is often not the most systematic and organized person among us. Agents all know what it is to write down names and phone numbers on scrapes of paper only to look at them later and wonder who the heck they are and what the heck they wanted. Or, you simply lose those scraps of paper all together. If you and I had half the money those scraps of paper represented, we'd be retired today! If you're like me, you've said aloud more than once, "if I'd ever get organized, I'd be dangerous." In fact I had a plaque that said, "I finally got it all together, but I forgot where I put it!" And the worst part about that is that I don't have any idea where that plaque is anymore.

The Freedom Funnel is about systematizing every section of what it takes to be a great, not just good. Contact to Client is no exception. When I started in real estate, a more experienced agent told me that when people showed some interest in buying or selling, he wanted to sink his talons into them as far as he could. That image freaks me out to this day. I get what he was saying, but I still think he watched too many creepy movies or something. At any rate, the point is well taken (pardon the pun). It is your job to be great, not good, at connecting with people when they show interest in real estate. And not just connect with them, but show them you are the person they need to know. A big part of that is your real estate training. Go get all the designations and certifications you can. Not just so you have the letters behind your name, but so you have the education they bring.

While you're getting that education, blog about it. Take pictures with you and your teachers. Write about the subject matter from the classes. Talk about real life situations where the knowledge mattered in the outcome for the client. Even if it was just a case study from the class, you write about it. Let people know you know you are smarter than the average bear about real estate. As you go through your practice of representing buyers and sellers, do a video blog post or two about how the knowledge you have helped to serve their best interests. Build content around you being a real estate expert! And use that content in your email campaigns with your contacts.

Your competition has not done this. They may have a blog or two on ten things to look for in a new house, or ten ways to maximize your sale. And you should have them too, but when you pull out all the content you created while taking the classes and the content you made while practicing the art and science of real estate, you win! They will see you as the go to expert they need to work with.

In addition to the real estate content, you need to be the go to expert for the market analysis they want. You need the training within your MLS to gather the data. The systems nowadays are phenomenal. But everyone has that. You also need to market the market you are analyzing. By that I mean, show them why this community is so wonderful. And you've already built out that content in the top of funnel material! You just have to connect the dots. No one you compete with will be able to touch you.

Where I live and practice, it is extremely easy to account for why some areas are higher rent than others: proximity to lakes, commerce, entertainment, etc. One of the big issues is ease of transportation too. Don't forget that one. The culture these days is all about walkable districts, and that's easily identifiable as a huge factor in property values here. Green spaces and bike lanes matter. Activities for children are big factors. And of course schools is the biggest one. Be careful how you address this one though. Just include links to independent sites so you can't be seen as steering anyone. And never, and I mean never, talk demographics as it relates to ethnicity. If you don't know why that's a third rail, then you need to retake the fair housing laws classes!

Contact to Client—Client Relationship Manager (CRM)

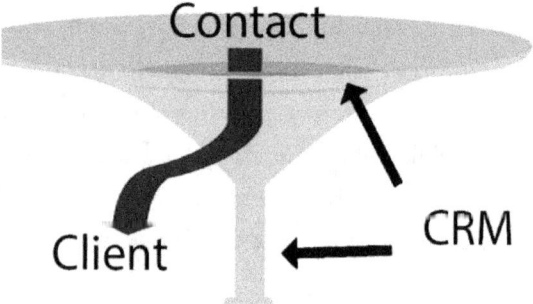

## CRM!!!

None of your hard work becoming a professional real estate agent or developing content that distinguishes you from the crowd matters without the right delivery system. I don't care how diligent and naturally organized you are, unless you're some sort of savant, you need a system. I've seen lots and lots of systems for Contact Relationship Manager (CRM) and most over promise and under deliver. Lots of them claim to have the best real estate scripts in the business, but they are extremely generic and written by people that clearly haven't ever practiced real estate.

Furthermore, the cheap real estate specific CRMs that are attached to websites or available to pay monthly to use, are often not as flexible as systems that are not real estate specific. The ability to almost think is what you want in your CRM. Is it flexible enough to change the content your contact will receive based on what they click on in the last communication? If it is, you have something worth working with. Pick one and learn it!

The ability to connect with your contacts when you are out showing houses or listing houses or working on your podcast is tremendous. With a CRM that has flexibility, you can be connecting them with content they are interested in and that shows you as the go to expert in your markets. Furthermore, the dashboard of that system will deliver your prospecting calls when it's time to prospect on the phone. It will deliver your tracking calls with your sellers and buyers when it's time to track with them. You learn that system, build out your campaigns with your content, time block accordingly and it will be your Freedom Train!

For instance, let's say a friend from the Chamber of Commerce Networking group you go to wants to ask you about real estate investing as a retirement plan. You ask him if it's ok to send some information regarding investing. He says he would like that so you start a campaign you built for Baby Boomers that need to super charge their investment portfolio with real estate investment. It's a combination of podcasts and blogs and real life examples of you helping people make money investing in real estate. The first email is very a brief blog showing how real estate flipping compares to the stock market for Return on Investment (ROI). You call them the next day to see if they read it and what their questions may be about it. If they haven't read it yet you tell them to read it and call you with any thoughts. Meanwhile, there's a next email already in place to send them in two days with a real life case study of someone you helped in their geographic area. It starts with, "I hope you thought the information I sent you was helpful. Here's a real life example of someone I helped recently with similar goals as you. Take a quick look and let's get together again soon to talk about it." A day after that second email goes out you call them and see if they want to grab a coffee. The next email is a discussion about where to get the funds to do investments. Is it a 25% down payment with a loan? Maybe they have cash they need to use somewhere. Or are they thinking a HELOC would be a good idea? Soon you'll be talking about tax strategies and looking for the right property to get started!

Consider the next sign call you get into the office. Someone saw the house at 123 Main and wonders how much it is. You do what you always do to interview them as they are asking you about the listing they saw. But this time, when you get their email and phone number, you do more than put them on an auto email from the MLS which may or may not get clicks. You enter them into the buyer campaign that you set up on your CRM too. They get an email that is a huge "Great talking with you today" email and you also write a handwritten note to drop in the snail mail (more on this later). Attached to the email you sent is a segment from the TV show or radio show or podcast of you leading a discussion about homeownership and it's long term effect to the economic well-being of those that "buy right." Then you see whether or not they clicked on that link when you call them back the next day to make sure they are getting the listings you sent and you ask them when they can come in for the free buyer consultation. Meanwhile, the next email is already on its way in a day or so with information about financing a home and some of the important factors that go into doing homeownership the "right way." In that email is a click to a spreadsheet that lets them figure out how much house they can afford. Buyer's all need to know that information.

I hope you get the point. A CRM done right can and will super charge your business and put you on the Freedom Train.

## Hand Written Notes

I mentioned hand written notes a moment ago. Use them. I interviewed the author of "7 Levels of Communication" on the radio show. In fact, I interviewed him twice. Michael Maher is his name. He emphasizes the use of hand written notes and I agree. Think about all the snail mail you throw away because it is computer generated junk mail. But if you get a hand written note in the mail you'll open it because it is such a rarity. In fact, what was the last hand written note you received that wasn't a birthday or holiday card? Maybe it was a thank you note from a wedding you attended? My daughter got married a year ago last spring and she faithfully wrote thank you notes to those that attended. One friend of mine said he attended three weddings last spring and hers was the only card he received. Hand written notes are rare and appreciated.

Build hand written notes into your campaigns. Your CRM will tell you when you need to write them. You just have to jot a few lines of appreciation. Here's the formula you should use. First name followed by, "it was great to [see or talk with] you." Then tell them something nice about them that you admire. There's always something to admire about everyone. Are they a great dad or a snappy dresser? Do they have a great work ethic or are they a good joke teller? Find something you admire in earnest and then the next line is how you wish you were more like them in that regard. Then tell them you look forward to seeing them or talking again soon. At the end, maybe in a p.s., let them know you're glad to help them in any way you can and for them to let you know how.

What is conspicuously missing is the ask for their real estate business. Don't ask. In fact, Maher says you shouldn't even send a branded card. Just have a generic note card or one of those "from the desk of" note cards. The goal is a relationship that deepens because you took the time to write them a note. Not that you wrote a note because you wanted something from them. That takes all the niceness out of it.

Consider receiving such a note. Someone told you it was great seeing you. They told you they admire you in some way. In fact, they told you they want to be more like you and they look forward to seeing you again. Then they offer to be of assistance to you any way they can and tell you to not hesitate to ask for the help. I'd not only open and read that card; I'd hold on to it in a file somewhere! I'd certainly have a fond notion of that person.

Now consider that card came from a high powered person showing you content you need to see. The content is from their podcast or blog article. It may even be a short segment from the TV or radio show that has the content you needed. That's the person that says they admire you somehow and wish they were more like you. That's powerful.

Now when you do get an appointment with them, you are positioned to have a consultation. You're not one of many having a listing presentation and trying to gain their business. You're the go to expert in their market consulting with them about their best interest. And you don't have to slash your commission to get the listing, and you don't have to take overpriced listings just so you have some. Look, we've all done it for one reason or another. We took a listing that we knew was overpriced because we thought we wanted our sign in that neighborhood or that we could at least pick up a buyer or two from the traffic the listing generates. But in the end, we always regret it. I still remember houses that didn't sell and I hate it. They don't call me anymore either. I'm too sheepish to call them. It's a bad deal for everyone.

I have one agent right now who is talking with a would be seller that had their listing expire because it was overpriced for its current condition. They spoke with three different agents. One of them told them the truth when they said, you can sell it in its current condition if you drop the price $60,000 dollars. Another told them that all they needed was new pictures and they'd sell it for the original price. They lied. My agent told them that they need to do some work on the house, retake great pictures and place it back on the market at their original list price. But I'm proud of my agent that he is unwilling to list it without either doing the work or dropping the price. It never ends well.

## Break Bread Together

Humans have been around a really long time. The ones that like each other have shared their food together for a very long time. It's a part of our evolutionary nature that breaking bread together is a relationship building activity. Some 10 plus years ago Keith Ferrazzi wrote the book, "Never Eat Alone." It says on the cover that it's about "how to build a lifelong community of colleagues, contacts, friends and mentors." I'd add to that clients. The act of sharing food together one on one and talking about their lives and goals are really important.

There are lots of chances in any given day to do that. You can have a breakfast, a mid morning coffee (I like tea myself), a lunch, a happy hour drink and a dinner. That's at least five times a day you can sit with someone and build relationship. But the best success I had with doing this is stacking those appointments so that the one that's finishing gets to meet the one that's leaving.

Have a breakfast and schedule a coffee in the same place with someone else right after it. When the one shows up and the other is leaving, they see that you are in demand. And try to schedule comparable people so that they respect the other person you're meeting with. If you've got a contact that wants an expensive new build, but the person they bump into is an fha buyer in the 80k range it could backfire a little. In fact both of them may feel like you're not the best guy (or gal) for them. But if they see someone they feel good about that you're meeting with, then you've accomplished the goal.

Do this at a place that people know you. Make it a place that feels like a second office to you. Also make it a place that will perform their service well. I had this blow up in my face once when I took some clients to the new sports bar the day the USA Soccer Team was playing to move on in the World Cup Tourney. The place was packed and the crowd was enthusiastic. But the kitchen and servers were overwhelmed. It didn't make for a good experience. Oh well, lesson learned. Take my advice and build some rapport with a local spot or two so this goes well for you. It can and will if you do.

*Real Talk Truth: Your goal is relationship AND establishing yourself as the go to expert. If you take seriously the community to contact work, you can build on it with the contact to client work much of which is done alone building content and campaigns for your CRM. But the goal is always face time.*

*Whatcha Gonna Do? Do you have ongoing systematic communication that is full of valuable content? Do you call your contacts regularly? Do you break bread with them regularly? Do you have personalized social media and email content featuring you as the go to expert in your market? Get all of the above.*

## Chapter 12
# Client to Contract

Client to Contract (Bottom of Funnel)

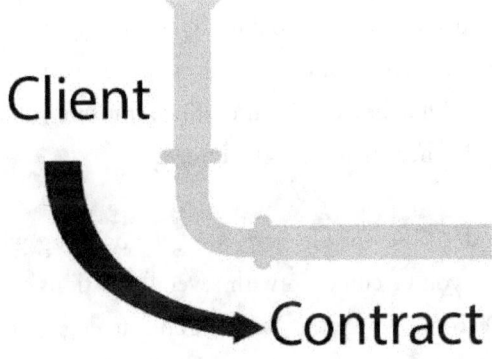

Now we're at the bottom of the funnel and it's game on. If this were football, I'd say you were in the Red Zone and it's time to score! You can't afford any negative plays now. No fumbles, interceptions or penalties. You've got to be operating out of your strengths now. If this isn't your strength, you need training camp all over again. Because this Client to Contract section is what your real estate license is all about. You can hire help and outsource much of the rest of the work. A closing coordinator can help you with contract to close. There are marketing firms that can take over most of your social media efforts in Community to Contact. In Client to Contract — it's all you!

Think about the last time you went to a doctor's office. Did you see the doctor as soon as you walked in? No? You saw a front desk worker that, amongst other things wanted to qualify you for the visit. They checked your insurance card or told you what the cash payment would be for the visit and likely collected it on the spot. Then they told you to take a seat in the first waiting room.

Was the next person you saw the doctor? No? You saw someone with a clipboard and a white coat or scrubs, but it wasn't a doctor. They took you back and took some vitals. They put you on a scale, you sucked in your gut and tried to have lighter thoughts, but you were still heavier than you wanted. Then they put you in the second waiting room. Oh, they call it an exam room, but you spend more time waiting in there than being examined.

Finally, the doctor comes in and you get how long with them? If you're smart, you've come up with several questions to ask to keep them in the room longer. If you're good at engaging them with thoughtful questions they'll become slightly more interested in you and actually engage their brains more. You might even want to have a really good joke to tell just to make it more human and gain their interest. I learned that uttering vowel sounds like uuuuuhh, or aaaaahh makes them wait to hear what could be coming out of my mouth next so they don't hurry up and leave while I'm thinking of the next question.

The point to the doctor reference here is that they have made business decisions that keep them moving from exam room to exam room focused on what they are licensed to do. No one else in that chain of interaction is licensed to do it. The doctor alone is. And you need to take a clue from what they're doing. I know, I know, we can't be as disinterested in our client's overall experience as they are in the patients, but the point is to recognize that you alone are licensed to write the contracts and open up the homes. You need to figure out how to staff and/or systematize as much of the other stuff as you can and focus on the client to contract work, and you better be great at it.

Client to Contract (Agent Sweet Spot)

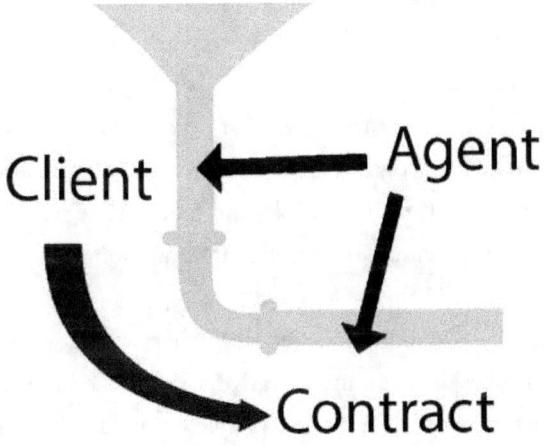

Now I have to back pedal some from the hyperbole that is that doctor's office example because everyone hates that about doctor's offices. Believe me, I don't want you to become a disinterested jerk. (My apologies to my doctor friends, but that's often what it feels like to us.) No, on the contrary, I've spent pages and pages here trying to help you figure out how to be quite the opposite. I've argued that you need to be about their lives beyond real estate. But you've also got to get your business set up so that you are concentrating on client to contract and getting the support you need from systems and staff.

Take a second to think about what keeps you from spending the bulk of your time on the revenue generating activity of client to contract activities. I'm guessing there are two main categories: lack of clients to spend time with and administrative tasks that pull you away from the clients you do have. Does that sound about right?

The last couple of chapters will change the lack of clients problem, but it will add other stuff to your daily tasks. That's fine, because if your problem is a lack of clients, you have time on your hands. The trick will be managing the situation when you go from doing everything yourself to hiring some help when you need to. And that hire is an administrative assistant! Don't even think about a different hire. Even if your strength is in organization and administration, you have to free yourself from the tasks and concentrate on the client to contract. That's what the doctor illustration is about.

I'm probably only talking to a very few when I say don't even think about a hire besides an administrative assistant because the people that are attracted to real estate are people oriented people. If you are a task oriented person and are tempted to make your first hire a buyer's agent so you can focus on the tasks that need to get done, you probably are either going to be the owner of the company in a very short time, or you need a different line of work. Of the two, it's probably that you need a different line of work. However, there are a rare few that are so systems oriented they can figure out how to focus on systems and take over. The problem is that most systems oriented people think they're that person and they're not.

So for the rest of you, If your problem is that you can't focus on client to contract because of all the tasks, you are either ready for your assistant or in desperate need of the next chapter. Don't turn there yet though because this is the most important chapter in any agent's business. This is your focus. This is the time to shine!

There's a quote that has been attributed to various coaches over the years so I have no idea who said it first. But it bears repeating (which is probably why so many coaches say it). "It is not the will to win that matters, but the will to prepare." When teams take the field to compete, everyone out there wants to win. But more often than not, it's the team that wanted it bad enough to work toward that moment harder than the other team that ends up winning.

*Real Talk Truth: Being prepared to win by getting the education, designations and certifications of a real estate professional AND grinding out the content and campaigns that help you reel in contacts are the keystone habits you need.*

*Whatcha Gonna Do? Are you truly prepared to win? Or are you making excuses about being too busy to train to win? Take the time right now to consider if you really have the client to contract education to be the top professional in your market. Also, think about your systems for turning seller, buyer, investor leads into clients. Are they as strong and automated as they should be?*

# Chapter 13
# Topside Hustle and Background Grind

Here in Detroit, we are proud of the rise and grind work ethic that built this town and continues to rebuild it into a 21$^{st}$ century example of what it is to redefine one's existence. Grinding in business pays off when the lights come on and you can show your hustle as in an athletic competition. Running sprints and shooting jump shots after practice isn't so you look good for beach season. It's so you can out hustle your opponent in the fourth quarter of the championship game. World class athletes aren't watching film at night of opponents instead of going out to the bar with friends so they can pat themselves on the back for being committed to their craft. It's so they can win!

You need to do the work of getting ready to win in this client to contract section. How well educated are you really in representing clients? How long ago did you take the classes you took on representing buyers and sellers? Have you taken them at all? Even if you have, you need to stay sharp. Take them again if it's been a while. There's a reason big league hitters still hit off a tee in practice. Remember me bringing up Tim Duncan? He's the one that retired from basketball as maybe the greatest power forward in history. Do you remember what I told you his nickname was? That's right, The Big Fundamental. It warrants saying again, greatness comes from doing the basics over and over with excellence.

I was recently in a class (practicing what I preach by taking classes still) and the teacher was a woman from the east coast that I respect as a very good business woman. She still is a practicing broker and is leading agents in the real world. She said something almost in passing that has stuck with me. She said to the brokers in the room, "don't try to train your own agents." She likened it to trying to teach your own teenagers. They don't listen. In fact, they hear the same thing you said somewhere else and come home to tell you what awesome thing they learned thereby proving they weren't listening to you when you said it.

The joke at the churches I worked at years ago was the expert in the room was the one that traveled the farthest to be in the meeting. It's an old saying that a prophet gets no respect in his hometown. All of this means that you and those you lead should take classes outside your offices. But that doesn't let you off the hook for doing homework inside your offices too.

That's the background grind part of the "you need a background grind and a topside hustle." The homework is on presentation and consultations. You need a significant breadth of talking points. And repetition matters. Practice the discussions you want to be great at. When someone asks you a question about how you're going to market their home if they ask you to list it, you need a rock and roll riff ready to go. And you need to be able to hit it hard without stuttering your way through it.

That reminds me of the story of "The Dream of the Blue Turtles." That was the title of the first solo album ever released by Sting back in 1985. It was released to rave reviews. I read an interview somewhere with the soon to become mega star known as Sting. In it the interviewer asked him what the difference was in working with jazz musicians instead of rock musicians. You see the album had all jazz greats in the band (except Sting). His answer fascinated me. He said the musicians on the album were all tremendously skilled, but he had to tell them something in order to get it right. He said that there is at least one huge difference between jazz and rock and roll: when the jazz musician starts a solo they often almost knock to get in and then they often play with a variation or two before they take over with their solo. But in rock and roll, Sting said, the soloist has to hit it hard from the jump. Once he articulated that distinction to the band it was great. They all, being great musicians, understood and applied what he said. The album was highly acclaimed and launched his now historic career.

The point to the Sting story is that you have to be rock and roll ready with every bit of your client to contract business. The only way to do that is to be prepared by the background grind of putting material together and reworking it several times. Then when the lights come on and it's time to shine, you are ready to hit your solo hard with the best riff you can. The background grind is meant to make your topside hustle be great.

I use "topside hustle" to talk about the need to be ready to hit the ground running when the opportunity presents itself. In today's attention deficit world, you need an answer right now when people have a question for you. It doesn't work to say, "let me get back to you on that after I've had a couple of days to research it." They'll find someone that can at least fake an answer right now and roll with them. Whether it's right or wrong, that's the world we're doing business in today. You need to have a market report ready when they want it. The background grind of having that knowledge at the ready will make your topside hustle effective when the lights come on and it's time to shine. That means you have to run reports in your markets at least once a week. Make it a habit.

Another is the inventory awareness. Walk through houses in the various price points in your market regularly. Even if you don't have a client to show it to, go alone. Know what $250,000 will buy in this neighborhood as opposed to that one. What does a half a million dollar house look like where you do business? What does a house have to have to be over one million where you are? If you're in some parts of the country it just has to have four walls and a roof, but where I am it is considerably more complicated than that. When you can say, "I was in three houses just like yours this past week that all sold between x and y, and none of them had the finishes yours has. Let me show you my market analysis I did this week on your area." Then you can write that exclusive right to sell contract up and land that listing. They believe you know what you're talking about because you put in the grind of creating reports and walking through listings on the way to or from the office.

You also need to read. So many of us have a need for speed but we need to read. We go through our life with the rpm gauge in the red. It's bad for your blood pressure, but it's horrible for your brain. You need to slow down and study. And I don't mean fluff stuff on the back of the toilet tank. I mean find solid books that will challenge you to be a better you. They will slow you down and build your brain. You will be deeper, more thoughtful and develop the gravitas you need to hold people's imaginations. Being able to quote an author and apply a thought from something you read is not expected from the real estate agent. When you do these things, you will differentiate yourself from the crowd. You will attract people to yourself if you do it naturally. The only way to get that in your life is through reading regularly. Turn off reality TV and the sports channels and read. I don't even watch my own show most of the time it's on.

There's a myriad of ways you need to apply the will to prepare as a background grind so your topside hustle is effective when it's time to shine. But let me say that one last thing you need to do is scout the competition.

There's a reason the great ones watch film of their opponents and break down their weaknesses. Now, in real estate you don't ever want to bad mouth anyone. Remember what Paul of Tarsus said about doing everything without complaining or grumbling. No, you just need to understand what you can emphasize to differentiate yourself from them. If you're a smaller independent like I am, then you have a personal touch that the big boys can't have. When I'm recruiting agents for instance, I talk about what a close knit group of agents we are and how we are all in it together. When I'm listing homes I talk about being a local expert tied into the local business and municipal government communities. I let them know my kids went through those schools and played ball in those parks. That shows the client that they have an advantage in working with me that the others don't have. You understand what I mean? Know you're competition so you can show you're different, not so you can talk them down. No one likes people who talk bad about others when they're not in the room. It makes us wonder what they'll say about us when we leave. Don't be that guy.

## Topside Hustle When it's Time to Shine

This is still about you, but it's the part of you that knows how to listen and land a lead. It's topside because it's the part people see. It's hustle because we live in a lightning fast world. When people want your attention, you need to be ready from the background grind to give it to them even if it's just scheduling an appointment to meet. But your CRM has to be tuned to keep them warm until that appointment happens.

You've got someone that wants to talk about selling their home or selling investment homes they own. That's two different appointments and you need a specific campaign for each already ready to send them. Maybe you have a lead regarding buyers. Are they moving up, right sizing, relocating to the area or are they investors? If they are investors, are they flippers or long term investors? You need content ready to go on all of these different scenarios. See what I mean about the key being the will to prepare? But all real estate transactions are similar in this one way: you need to know their why! Understanding motivation is the key to winning in the client to contract section.

I recently helped three sets of buyers. One was a relocation family from out of state. One was a soon to be married couple, and one was a couple expecting their first child. It was vital I learned their real motivations because that is the controlling factor. When I say controlling factor, I mean it is what they are organizing their decisions around. It will determine what and where they buy. And they won't typically tell you what it is. You have to discover it as you go. The better you are at discovering their real motivation, the better you are at helping them. The problem is that they often don't know themselves, or it's fluid and shifts on them.

The relocation was a family of four that contacted me through one of my websites and I reeled them in on the phone. The interesting part of their story was that she was a real estate agent that didn't use her license much because she worked for a bank. The original story was, that he was taking a job in Lansing (Michigan's capital) working with the state. Lansing is 86 miles west of my office. But she was transferring to Madison Heights which is five miles east of my office. So they wanted to split the difference and find a strong school district about 30-40 miles west of my office. That's further away than I normally go, but I wanted to help. Their story changed several more times before we were through. She ended up with a job in Lansing too and they bought northwest of Lansing about 100 miles from my office! Their motivation was way different in the end than it was in the beginning. But it was because their circumstances shifted.

The soon to be married couple was a second marriage for both. She was the preapproved buyer coming from a lender referral. (Yes, you should get referrals from lenders not just give them.) She opened with, "it has to be Birmingham Schools." Her young son was enrolled in that school district. But that district is pricy for our area and the square footage she could purchase there wasn't what she wanted. She sent me a For Sale By Owner listing from Zillow in a different school district and we got it done for her. The real talk truth of it was that the new husband lived in a much bigger home with his first wife and she didn't want to be the one that made him downsize so much. But that's hard to talk about with a new client so it had to be discovered as we went along. In the end though, we were able to extend the rental agreement inside the desired district an extra month and satisfy the school's requirements. But the real talk truth was not where we started. I'm not sure she understood what was really driving her right up to the end.

The couple expecting their first child took a few showings to figure out. She was very talkative. He was not. They wanted a ranch style home with a basement and preferably 2 and a half baths. The half bath should be in the basement or at the top of the basement stairs. Every time we entered a home to view it, he would go straight down the basement. I was trying to get him to talk so I would follow him. I thought we were looking at furnaces and plumbing and electrical boxes, you know, guy stuff. But he only asked me about moisture in the basement. He didn't seem interested in anything else. About the fourth house I asked what was important about a dry basement? The in home music studio was his answer! He is a professional musician. In fact, as I write this, he's in the UK on tour. The only thing that mattered to him was a place to work. She wanted the half bath downstairs to prevent the musicians from trapesing through the house at baby's nap time, etc. Find motivation and find the controlling factor in decision making.

All of those stories are about being great at helping people discover their motivation as you travel with them because they often don't really know when they start out. It is not easy, but the better you are at it, the easier your job becomes. So have the habit of asking the next question. The buyer says they want a big backyard. Ask, "what's important about a big backyard?" "I like to garden" might be the answer. But don't stop yet. "That's awesome, what's important about gardening to you?" "My grandfather taught me to garden when I was a child and it was some of the happiest times of my life. My daughter has a three year old and is expecting their second child this spring. I want to have the three year old outside with me while she has to tend to the newborn" could be the answer. Now you're getting somewhere. Now you're understanding motivation. Not only will you help them faster, you'll help them better. Stay in touch. Send them a note or two about gardening and get their referrals for years!

It's the same thing with sellers. They're not usually quite as hard to sort out though. If you're selling your house, you probably know why. You've got another child on the way. There's a new job in another area. You've lost a job and can't afford it anymore. The marriage is ending. The kids are grown and the house is more house than you want now. You're cashing out your investments. There are a lot of possible answers to why sellers are selling, but they usually understand them. And all sellers want the same things: the most money, in the least time, with the least hassle. And when you understand the motivation, you understand the controlling factors. Now you can take control.

## Selling the Sellers

You already know phrases like, "if you list, you last." Or the idea that it's much easier to work with 20 sellers at once than it is to work with 20 buyers at the same time. You can only show so many houses in a given week, but others can show your listings every day. So we want to work with sellers. But how do we get sellers to work with us when it's time to turn them into listing contracts? You've got to be able to sell the seller on the idea of you.

You may have heard that sellers want to work with a strong agent. It's true. They want someone that is in control and understands how to get them what they want. You need to look and sound like you're that agent. I had heard that, but I learned it the hard way. You see, most of us start our career working more with buyers. If we're good at it, we learn to be intuitive and flexible with them. We help them understand themselves through the journey of shopping for and closing on a home. But that intuitive, flexible approach doesn't work with sellers. It worked on buyers because they wanted to feel in control and we have to help them feel that way. They don't want to feel as if you are leading them down a path at all. They want to feel as though things went as they envisioned them going in their buying adventure.

Sellers want no part of adventure. They don't want intuition and flexible. They want systematic and sure! This one point is why most agents are not good at both the seller side and the buyer side. It's hard to be touchy, feely with buyers one minute and cold and calculated with sellers the next. But that's the job. You need the background grind of creating a selling system and the rock and roll riffs that communicate it wonderfully.

It starts with your marketing to sellers. What is your messaging like in regards to your business. It is probably either buyer oriented or seller oriented. You need both. Make sure you have messaging regarding your real estate practice that appeals to buyers and sellers. With sellers it's about systems that sell and the confidence you project about those systems and your abilities. Buyers are interested in the houses, but sellers are interested in their market and in you. Do you inspire confidence in them?

"When we list your home, we will sell it on average, in 26.5 days." I happen to run that average days on market just yesterday for some marketing I'm doing so that's a real number. The fact that it is less than 30 days is great, but it is the third most important thing in that sentence. The first two, in order of importance, are the phrases "we will sell it" and "when we list your home." The first inspires confidence in you and the second assumes an answer to the question of if we are listing their home.

Statements that assume the answers to prior questions are tried and true techniques in sales. But be careful with techniques. Everyone hates to feel manipulated. Don't try to technique people into listing. You don't inspire confidence that way. You come across as untrustworthy. Tell people what you do to sell homes and why you do it. Let them see that you understand what it takes to get them the best price in the least time with the least hassle. And tell them directly. Don't beat around the bush.

If they have murals of clouds on their ceilings, tell them it will hurt their bottom line. If the first thing you smell when you walk in is the kitty litter box, tell them that will cost them money. If they have every closet stuffed full, tell them they'll come out ahead renting a storage locker or moving it to their friend's garage for now. There are plenty of places to get all the seller tips you want. There's no need for me to list them here. My job is to tell you the *Real Talk Truth: strong and direct statements will gain their confidence and win you listings.*

I'm not going to give you some alpha of the pack garbage as to why strength and directness wins listings. That may work with some, but it'll backfire with most. Don't march around their house like you're in charge. No, you need humility when it comes to your relationship with them. Let them know you understand this is a job interview and you're applying for the job of being their agent. Humility in terms of relationship is vital, but confidence in terms of ability is too.

Persuading people that you are the agent of choice in their market is an art. The art of persuasion was first talked about by the ancients as

The Art of Rhetoric. Rhetoric, to the ancients was about public speaking, but we can update it here for our purposes to be about presentation and messaging. Keep in mind that if you do what we talked about in the previous chapters, you will have quite an online presence. You might say an online persona. So the persuasion has already started by the time you're talking to anyone about selling their home. And with the online persona I've laid out for you (especially in the middle of the funnel) you have a tremendous advantage. It's important you don't mess that up with any sort of cockiness. You need to understand the three parts of rhetoric: Ethos, Pathos and Logos.

Ethos has to do with your standing in the community. It looks and sounds like ethics because it is about their perception of you as a good person for the job or not. We talk about ethos when we say, "people do business with those they know, like and trust." Believe me when I tell you that in the 21$^{st}$ century they are already persuaded one way or the other before you talk to them because of your online presence or lack thereof. If you're doing what I've been telling you to do, you're winning big time already. So don't mess it up. Be nice, be polite, be humble, but be ready for the opportunity to talk about selling their home. Be ready for your rock and roll solos and hit it hard with enthusiasm.

Ethos is more than the meeting. It's the reputation before the meeting. For instance, if you were looking for a marriage counselor you wouldn't pick OJ Simpson. He's not thought of as the man for the job. If you wanted a General Manager for a football team you wouldn't pick Matt Millan. He famously drove the Detroit Lions to the worst season in history. They didn't win a single game. They finished 0-16. They are the only team in history to lose every game. Under his leadership, they put the "less" in "winless."

Your standing in the community matters. So does how you present yourself. This depends entirely on your community. I sell houses in Metro Detroit. I drive a Chevy! I could drive a foreign car. Lots of people in the Detroit area do. They talk about the fact that cars are global these days. And it's true that the car I drive wasn't built in Detroit. But the people I serve around here either make their living from the big three or their parents did or their friends and neighbors do. We've watched too many people suffer at the hands of global manufacturing and I'll be damned if I'm going around in a Toyota in front of them. My Chevy isn't going to win me any listings, but it sure as hell isn't losing me any either.

I drive a Chevy not a Caddie. I work in areas where working people live. I wear blue jeans with suit coats and I don't wear jewelry besides my wedding ring. It's who I am and it's where I'm from. I also have a Master's in Philosophy and write books and have a TV show. But I try to be sure I lead with that which identifies with the people I serve. Don't get it twisted. Most of them are college graduates and earn their living as professionals, but they are Detroit professionals not LA or NYC professionals. You need to be the person you are for the people you serve. Pay attention to that. I assure you, they do even if it is only subconsciously.

Ethos has to do with what you say too. Point out that your job is to bring them the knowledge your professional development has brought you in preparing, staging, pricing, marketing and negotiating the sale of their home. Again, give them the real talk truth regarding the condition of their home. I recently walked through a perspective listing with a woman that had five different colors of paint and three different types of flooring within view of their front door. She had heard that taking down family photos to depersonalize the home when selling was a good idea, but living in that home day to day, it never occurred to her how personalized her decor was. I literally took her to five other homes for sale in our area to drive the point home. I took her to two flips and three new builds. At each home I told her that these people are professional home sellers and she should note the decor. She painted her home in preparation for sale. It probably increased her sale $20,000. Her husband is a home contractor so it cost them a little time and less than three hundred dollars in supplies.

The point to the last story is to tell them the real talk truth about their situation. You are the professional home seller in the room. They watch HGTV and think they know what it takes to sell homes. They look at Zillow and see that the neighbor's sold for x. They think they know what they need to know. You've got to be strong and explain why you do what you do, AND how it will benefit them!

This brings us to Pathos. It looks like empathy and sympathy because pathos has to do with feelings. Every good preacher and politician knows that if you're going to persuade anybody about anything, you need to move them emotionally. That's why they all tell real life stories. At least they claim they are real life stories. It's why Presidents bring war heroes to the State of The Union address and why you need client testimonies. You need them on your website and social media channels. But you also need to tell those personal stories as illustrations of the points you're making. Remember, every seller has three objectives: the highest price, in the least time, with the least hassle. Speak to those points in stories.

Every seller has some personal motivation as well. Are they finally retiring and ready to move to a warmer climate? Tell them stories about your last vacation at the beach or your last golf trip. Do they want more space for their growing family? Tell them about the client you just helped to make that move and how not sharing bedrooms has led to less strife in the house. Are they selling to get closer to the job so they spend less time in the car and more time with their kids? Tell them about coaching your kids t-ball or soccer team. Move their emotions with stories and show them how you are going to help them achieve their goals through preparing, staging, pricing, marketing and negotiating the sale of their home!

Logos is the final part of persuasion and it has to do with logic and reason. If you've done the things I've told you to do in the preceding paragraphs, you're golden on Logos. 21$^{st}$ century America is not primarily rational. I mean, just look at elections. It's Pathos based with attacks on and defenses of Ethos. Logos only comes into play in terms of talking points designed to give a sense of logic. It's as if logic is just hinted at enough to make us feel a little bit rational which means it's really a matter of Pathos. How else do you explain 2016 elections? Fake news and little or no logos won the day.

But we're dealing with people's homes and their money you say. Surely we are more rational about those things than we are about elections. You're right. But if you do what I've been saying—tell them what you're going to do for them and why you're going to do it, you will win on logos too. I wish we were deeper than that as a people, but we're not. If you come across the exception to this, just be ready to go deeper on the five points: prepping, staging, pricing, marketing and negotiating the sale of their home.

Prepping is largely about deferred maintenance. Look, we all live in homes and don't always wipe all the finger prints around the light switches, or clean the baseboards. It may have been a while since you weeded the garden or put a fresh coat of paint on the front door. My classic story is the doorknob on the door to the basement at my house. It's an older house and the handle gets loose. To open it you kind of lift a little while you turn it. I live there and have done it thousands of times. I don't think about it. It's just how you open that door. But when a potential buyer gets to that door, it won't just open for them. The psychology of that moment is, to them, a sense that this house is broken. But my house isn't on the market right now. I assure you, if it was, there would be a new doorknob there!

Back to the front door and garden. Everyone knows that curb appeal matters supremely. First impressions are lasting impressions. Maybe you know that a new front door is consistently the biggest return on investment in NAR's annual study regarding what repairs and improvements pay off. Deferred maintenance on front door paint is a classic problem. People are carrying packages and kicking the door open all the time. Scuff marks cost the seller money. Sorry, but we are that shallow as a people. Now couple that with the 30 seconds it takes for the buyer's agent to open a lockbox and get the buyer in the front door. The buyers are looking over the edge of the porch into the flower garden while they wait. If they are looking at weeds, it could be game over before they get in the door. Prepping a home for sale is huge! There's lots more to say about prepping, but let's look at staging too.

Staging is after prepping and is about making it appear as if it is the sort of place that has never been cluttered and will never be cluttered. It has to look magazine photo ready at all times. In almost every case, that means taking things away as much as anything. The same lady with five colors of paint and three kinds of flooring had way too much furniture. The site lines were full of obstacles and we had to open up the layout by removing and rearranging furniture. But get the docs signed first because if you do it right, they'll want to keep living there!

Pricing is everything and you already know that. Speak authoritatively to it. Tell them that if they price it just 15% over market value they will cut out 90% of the buyers from viewing their home. Show them the real comps and tell them that days on market are their enemy. Have examples of homes that sold for less than they should have because the seller tried to get more than they should have. But also tell them that you are committed to NOT letting their house steal their money. For most of our sellers, they have a significant part of their money in their house. Tell them you won't let their house keep their equity. Tell them your job is to make sure they don't leave their money on the table. Emphasize that the number one way people leave their money behind is by not prepping properly, not staging seriously and over pricing which creates days on market and that unholy trinity steals their money!

Now we're to marketing. Have a riff ready. Know your 13 point, 18 point, 21 point (whatever it is) marketing plan cold. Explain why you include professional photos free in all of your listings. Show them your days on market average beats the MLS days on market average severely. Let them know that if the home doesn't sell in the first 21 days, you will schedule an open house with one of your hand-picked agents. Tell them that if their home doesn't sell in the first 60 days you will reduce your listing side commission and add it to the buyer's agent commission. And remind them that the systems you use are the most powerful in the industry, but you have the advantage of being well known through your use of media so your listings will be viewed by more than other agent's listings. Be bold! Sellers want a strong and confident agent. So be one. Just don't be a jerk while you do it.

Share with them stories of successful negotiating and how much you enjoy helping people get the best deal possible on the sale of their home. Be sure to manage expectations up front, and let them know that a successful negotiation is one where both parties are equally unhappy because no one gets everything they want. Show them you are a Certified Negotiation Expert, and if you're not yet, become one. Mention that negotiation is about terms and conditions, but it's also about time. Remember there are three things sellers all want: best price, least time and least amount of hassle.

*Real Talk truth: Whether it's with buyers or sellers, client to contract is your time to shine. It is time for your topside hustle to be on display. It is game time and the lights are on. But it's your background grind game that will prepare you to win. It's the discipline to be prepared when the contact moves to client that will bring you the freedom to live the life you envision.*

*Whatcha Gonna Do? Create the marketing plan complete with success stories (testimonies) and practice your rock and roll riffs. Know how to ask questions that uncover the real motivations. Be the best educated and articulate agent in your market. Remember that hard work beats talent when talent fails to work hard.*

## Chapter 14
# Contract to Close

Contract to Closing

Contract ➡ Closing

"The job is never finished until the paper work is done." Those were the words on a poster in my neighbor's bathroom when I was a kid. I got the joke back then. The dual meaning: in a business world you have paperwork to process, and in a bathroom... Well, you get it too. But when I got into real estate, I really got it because there were no paychecks until all the paperwork was completely done! There's no paycheck every two weeks or once a month. You have to close to get cash in real estate.

When I first got started there was a gruff old agent in the office. I remember him saying in a meeting that when he got a contract signed he threw it in a drawer and waited for the closing. He said it was the lender's and title company's job to take care of it from there. He just waited for the phone call to tell him there was a clear to close. I thought that was the dumbest thing I had ever heard. Okay, not really, but it wasn't smart. To be fair, his point was that he needed to go find the next deal. He wanted to be focused on the pipeline, and I think that's a great idea. But trusting others with your paycheck is a bad idea. I tell my agents that about 30% of your job is making sure everyone else does their job. Furthermore, your job of building relationships that lead to referrals is about to get even easier so don't miss the chance.

Keep in mind you are building a business that brings you freedom. The quality of the experience for your client can go down the tubes big time still. We've all had nightmares after the contracts are signed before the deal has closed that have soured it for our clients. That's how you lose future business to say nothing of the hard work you have in on that deal not paying off. No, you have to be good at contract to close too.

If you're the task oriented and organized type it will be instinctual and natural, but if you are the people oriented person that most agents are, you'll not enjoy it as much so you need to systematize and staff up. In that order by the way. Before you have business enough to staff up with an administrative assistant, you need a system that makes sure things are not falling through the cracks and your people are communicated with regularly. You need a transaction tracking system that makes sure everything gets done including the task of keeping your clients informed and happy. And you need to understand the system enough that when you hire that first assistant, you can give them the system and the training they need to be effective. Furthermore, you can explain, with passion, why it's so important. Your admin help needs to know that this is about people and their experience of working with you not just getting tasks completed. Mind you, tasks not completed will ruin the experience of working with you, but the experience the client is having needs to be the focus. Even the contract to close section is about your relationship with your people!

Contract to Closing (Transaction Tracker)

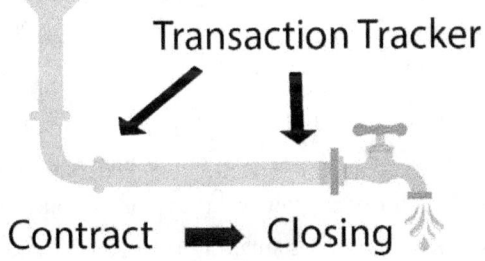

The key to doing this really well is to look at it as built in opportunities to build relationship between you and your clients. Set up your tracking system so everything that happens is an email, a handwritten note, a phone call or a photo opp. If you really want to turn it up a notch, find the biggest areas of interest and turn those into social media posts.

Take a seller for instance. You've just signed a new listing agreement and the listing is going live in three or four days. You take some initial cell phone quality pics and post a coming soon status on facebook, twitter, Instagram, etc. But you also mention that you're there with your new client going over a prepping consultation and mention a couple of the items you pointed out. Just today I was helping an old client of mine think about selling their mom's house. It needs updates, but is otherwise a well maintained home. The kids all agree they don't want to pour any money into updating the home, but I know they'll get a better price by playing a little defense. By that I mean they should look at mitigating the biggest negatives in the home. The two that are the top of the list are the faded front door paint and the dingy basement. So the social media post is before and after photos of a basement. The photos aren't even their basement. I don't have after photos of their basement yet. The photos are of a basement that is dirty and dingy and poorly lighted but was spruced up by removing all of the contents, freshly painting it and getting really bright LED lighting. They are nice blue/white bulbs instead of the old yellow bulbs. It's quite a contrast. The text is, "Had a prep session with our new clients today. It's amazing what a little prepping a home for sale can do for your bottom line." Don't bother asking for business there. You're just making sure you hit them with high impact photos and a brief message that keeps you top of mind regarding real estate. You're just taking advantage of the attraction of action.

When the marketing is ready, send it to your client. Let them see the single property website, the email flyer, the links to social media and all the websites their listing can be found on. They need to know your professional photographer has made their home look beautiful online. Then call them and point out what you sent. Be excited about what a great job your marketing does attracting buyers. People need to be told what a great job you're doing for them. Your voice inflection and word choices make a remarkable difference in how people feel. Use that when you're talking about your services. The human being reacts to that. Think about the type of voice you use with kids to be positive. It's higher pitched than your normal voice, it sounds like you're smiling (because you are) and it goes up at the end of sentences. Use a paired down version of that voice when you talk about the marketing material with them.

When the listing is live, it will get some initial traffic as new listings do. Make sure you communicate with the seller about every showing. Even your out of town sellers should get an automated email about the showings. Our system lets them get buyer agent feedback automatically too. But it's your job to communicate with your people. Don't let a couple of words from a different agent be your excuse for not doing your part. Buyer agent feedback is not enough especially if their words are negative. That will be a huge downer. Don't let that vibe linger. You are associated with those words and that vibe because you are their agent.

Pick a day and make sure all of your sellers hear from you that day. Tuesdays can be more than taco days. Call them every Tuesday and talk about the feedback. Let them know you've had 19 showings in 2 weeks and 0 offers. That points to two issues: the condition and the price. Be proactive with your sellers. We've all heard it in seminars before: the number one complaint about selling agents is that they listed the home and I haven't heard from them. Remember, you've got your clients most prized possession in your hands. You better be in touch with them about it at least weekly by phone.

There are showings, but what else do sellers need to know? Is their home on the market in a vacuum? No! Show them updated market reports. Hopefully you showed them comparable sales when you initially talked to them about their home. Have any of the actives gone pending? Have any of the pendings closed? Have there been any new listings or price changes on existing listings? Keep your clients well informed about their listing and the surrounding market. Make sure every one of those conversations have genuine human interaction. I just got off the phone with a seller client about the counter offer we sent a buyer. But I also asked him about his mom's hot water heater in another town because he was helping her get a new one last time I talked to him. In this conversation, he mentioned he had to take his kids to a school function. Guess what I'll ask him about next time I talk to him.

I'm not going to walk you through every step on the list. Just think about it as if you are trying your best to create relationship with this person and you're looking for excuses to communicate with them. You'll find scores of reasons to touch base with your sellers if you take that one concept seriously. It has to be automated though. You can't possibly keep all of this straight in your head. Use a software system that is made for real estate transactions. A great CRM can be used too. You can set up your CRM to be a transaction tracker if you want, but there are plenty of transaction trackers out there and some are very affordable. You need to log in daily and actually do everything there for you to do. That goes for sellers and buyers too.

That brings us to an important point. There will come a time, fairly soon, that you can't be in touch with everyone. You've got transactions in the pipeline that need your attention, you've got clients you're working with that you better give your attention and you've got relationships and networking to do. What's the priority? I'm glad you asked. It is in this order: the client to contract section (remember this is what your license is good for), the contact to client section, the continued client relationship section, the community to contact section and then the contract to closing section. Contract to closing is last on the list because it's the first one you give up. But you better have a great hire here. Make sure your administrative help understands that this is all about the experience for the client not just getting the task done. I think it helps to make the number one task the client's positive experience. That way it's clear.

Your contract to close section is a conveyor belt on the way to the closing table. This section has very important deadlines that must be met the right way. It often involves addenda and renegotiations. Those are your tasks as the licensed agent. A licensed assistant can help with document preparation and communication, but you should still be involved. Make sure the clients all understand the deadlines and implications. Your automated emails should be a primer on this subject early and often. Nothing will sour the experience more than problems in this section. They have high expectations and are on edge during this time. Every little glitch feels like a big deal to them. Do not poo poo their concerns. It will backfire on you if you try.

Think of it as bedside manner in a hospital. They are getting news they may not fully understand so you need to communicate it well. Keep your voice inflection, your body language and facial expressions in mind. In my office we call the glitches that come up "minor real estate emergencies." We see them every day so they are minor, but to the client they are a really big deal. Their money and their home are on the line at the same time. That's huge. I liken it to the emergency room at the hospital. For the patient it is a crisis. For the staff and doctors it's Thursday. But we don't get to have the same nonchalance they have. Think about it. The emergency room doesn't need referrals, but we do! Take it all very seriously. Don't you dare throw the file in a drawer and wait for a clear to close. Have a system that you work every day.

*Real Talk Truth: Contract to close can sour your relationship as easily as any place around The Freedom Funnel cycle, but you can use it powerfully to build relationship through proactive communication.*

*Whatcha Gonna Do? Make sure you have an infographic explaining the closing process and communicate proactively each step of the way. Practice the right inflection and facial expressions when having to explain bumps on the road to closing.*

# Chapter 15
## Budget Bucket

Your Freedom is in Your Budget

Cash

Budget Bucket

You need a budget bucket. If the image of a funnel leading to a faucet makes sense, then you need a bucket ready to catch the cash. Don't get distracted now. The whole point here is to achieve freedom. Keep your eyes on the prize and get there. We need to look at your budget bucket because it's not how much you make but how much you keep and what it cost to get it that matters in any business venture. You've probably heard the urban myth, at least I hope it's an urban myth, about the top producing agent that broke down in tears at the award ceremony because they'd produced plenty but had little to show for it. They're handed an award and tissue. I've gotten awards. You can't retire on awards.

Early on in my career, I was at one of those regional award banquet things for a big brand you've all heard of. The last award of the day was going to the top listing agent in the region that included the entire state of Michigan and the northern section of Ohio. The thing was dragging on and I had an appointment to go sell a house so I told the regional director dude that I had to split. He said, "you can't go. You're in the running for the biggest award of the day." "I have an appointment to sell a house" was my response. He looked at me very seriously and said quietly, "no, really, you won. You need to stay and receive the award." "Does it come with a check?" I asked. "No, but it comes with a $50 gas card" he said smiling as if that were meaningful somehow. I shook his hand and walked out. Someone received the award on my behalf, and I sold another house. I got the gas card too.

Generating revenue is way more important than spraining your shoulder patting yourself on the back. But what you do with that revenue will make or break your freedom. Your Budget bucket needs to be set up now! Begin with the end in mind. You didn't start a real estate career to have a job that pays periodically. You started in real estate to create a business that brought you the financial freedom that leads to true freedom. Suddenly I have that scene in mind from Braveheart where Mel Gibson's character screams the battle cry with a hokey accent on extreme close up, "F-R-E-E-D-O-M!!!"

We started our real estate career because we wanted freedom to work varied hours, freedom to not be tied to a desk, freedom to not be tied to a boss, freedom to work with people we like and freedom to be available to people we love. But we found out real estate is varied and complex, and above all else it's entrepreneurial! Have you heard the definition of an entrepreneur that says, "an entrepreneur is one willing to work 80 hours a week so they don't have to take a job working 40 hours a week!" Most of you reading this right now know that definition all too well.

Last night I had an appointment with a man I've known for years that is contemplating a career change. I met him because we coached a baseball team together when our sons were like 9 years old. They're both freshman in college now. He loves coaching kids. He still coaches baseball and football. In fact we're coached tournament teams together last summer. But he hates his job right now. He's tied to a desk and tied to a boss and not available to his kids every day from 8am to 4:30pm. The kicker is, no matter how good he is at his job, he makes the same money.

We met last night over the notion of flipping that script so he can have the life he wants. So I asked him, "dad to dad, how much money do you need regularly rolling in to be able to make the change and quit that job?" He told me his number and I warned him, "there will be some low hanging fruit when you get started. People who know and like you will gladly refer you. Someone's nephew will be looking to buy and someone's grandmother will be ready to sell. But don't rush into fool's gold and quit too fast. It'll take some time to build the business you can count on and one day retire on. But you can, and I believe will do it and I'll show you how." He appreciated the real talk truth of that.

Let's take a look at some more real talk truth. If you don't approach this thing with a budget bucket firmly established, you will fall into the trap of spending too much when things go well and not investing in your freedom when you should. And don't try to build it on debt. Let me say that again only emphatically. Don't try to build it on debt! See, the exclamation point means I mean it.

If you build your business on debt, even if it is a huge capital investment by you, you'll have a hole in your bucket dear Liza dear Liza. There's two ways to get a business: you can buy it or earn it. I suggest earning it. If you've got a capital investment to buy your business, you can. But please don't borrow the money for investing in your business. You can lead with revenue!

Once you have revenue. You need to Gain STEAM.

S –Stands for Savings (Pay your Freedom First!)
I don't care what business you're in—Pay Your Freedom First! We pay our rent first. We pay our car note first. We pay our entertainment first and hope there's some money to save and invest one day magically. That's crazy! Pay your Freedom First! Put your freedom in the budget as the first payment every time. Then figure the rent and the car and everything else around that!

T-Stands for Taxes.
After you pay your freedom, pay your Uncle Sam because there's no freedom if Sammie isn't paid! Have a quarterly payment figured out so it doesn't trip you up later. See a CPA about this so you don't have to see a tax attorney later. Oh, I've got horror stories on that.

E-Stands for Employees.
That includes you. Put yourself on a budget and pay yourself a reasonable salary. Don't have a great month or two and allow yourself to spend too much. There will be months that aren't so great. Be prepared for that.

A-Stands for Accounting.
To be successful, you have to be good at doing the business and

accounting for the money. No one starts a real estate business in order to be able to do the accounting for it. In fact, not even people that start accounting businesses do that. If it's a strength of yours, GREAT! If it isn't, find the help you need so it doesn't beat you.

M-Stands for Marketing.
You have to reinvest in your real estate business regarding marketing. Not everyone is awesome at it. You can find systems and services that can help you. But to Gain STEAM, you have to invest in marketing. The top of funnel activities will get you to a certain point, but reinvest in more as you go.

There's so much more to say about all of those, but I need to talk to you about Savings and paying your freedom first because that really is the point after all. The 'S' in Savings works well for the acronym in Gain STEAM. But there's a lot more to it than just putting 15-20% of each paycheck into a savings account. Your American Dream of a debt free life in a paid for house and being able to retire at a reasonable age is way more complicated than that. I've told Tina many times that I don't need any more than what we have. I just want to maintain what I have. We live in a humble home in a great area, we travel significantly, I have the freedom to sit and write these words on a Thursday at 11am. Life is good. But there are rainy days ahead too. One preacher friend of mine is fond of the saying, "you're either going through a storm in life, just got out of one or you're fixing to go into one." That's real talk truth too. Part of your American Dream is about building a future, and part of it needs to be about defending it. If you want the kind of riches that bring about freedom, you need RICHES!

R-Stands for Retirement Planning.

Retirement planning is more complex than having money stacked somewhere. Is it stacked in the right places and in the right ways? Is your home paid off when your income is reduced in retirement. Do you have the right health care figured out, etc.

I-Stands for Investment Planning.

Investment plans vary widely from person to person and time to time. I distinctly remember the '80s and Mutual Funds. Then there were other "products" the financial industry drummed up. Some of which crashed the global economy not that long ago. One friend of mine, who is a wizard at investing, says he recommends people invest in what they know. He grew up in the Detroit area and has always loved cars so he invests in automotive stuff. I know real estate so I invest there. You need a plan.

C-Stands for Cash Flow Issues.

This isn't complicated. Spend less than you make every month. Amen. Choir sing, end of sermon. Oh, it sounds simple, but... You have to take that seriously every day for the rest of your life. Housing is a big part of that. The recent crash made a lot of people press the reset button. Foreclosure and bankruptcy were everywhere. One family I met moved all three grown children and the mom into a house they bought with cash from pooling their resources. Then they continued to pool their resources and bought another one with cash for the oldest sibling. Then they did it two more times. That was a tough decision to move in together like that, but they did it and they won! Make the tough decisions about your cash flow and pay your freedom first!

H-Stands for Have Adequate Insurance.

Look these acronyms are tough so give me a break on H. But here's where we begin to play a little defense. August 11th 2014 it started to rain a lot here. By the time it stopped the sewer system was overwhelmed and tens of thousands of homes had sewer water in their basements including mine. That's when everyone learned that sewer backup is an additional rider on your homeowner's policy. It isn't covered without spending about $10-12 extra dollars a month on that rider. A little sewer water in the basement is disgusting but it didn't ruin my life. Other bigger problems could. Talk to insurance professionals and get the whole story of what you should carry.

E-Stands for Estate Planning.

There is no sense building your American Dream only to have the government get involved when you pass away. And you're doing no one in your family any favors by not having proper arrangements made for your assets. It's more complicated than it used to be. Consider, for instance, intellectual assets. Ask Prince's survivors. He died suddenly without adequate estate planning. Think too of medical directives. Please take that weight off your loved ones and see an Elder Law attorney.

S-Stands for Strategies for Taxes.

As you go, you need the right advice about taxes. Uncle Sam will shut down your freedom faster than anyone. Are you managing your income and tax liabilities well? Are you finding the right pre-tax products for your retirement planning? Do you have the professional advice you need to make the right choices? Are you managing your income and tax liabilities proactively, or are you just taking it as it comes and allowing Uncle Sam to do the same? Get it figured out now!

A financial planner friend of mine was on Michigan Real talk TV with us recently talking about the Rule of 72. Have you heard of it? It's really simple, but like all simple truths when it is correctly applied, it has profound results. The Rule of 72 states that you can determine the length of time it will take to double your money by dividing the number 72 by the rate of return. So, if you can get a return on your money of 10% a year. You can double your money in 7.2 years. A 12% rate of return means you'll double your money in 6 years. This is huge when you think about how many such periods of your life are likely in front of you. I wish someone had driven this home to me when I was 20 years old.

If a 20 year old sets aside $2000 dollars a year and can get a 10% rate of return on that money, they will accumulate over 1.8 million dollars by the time they are 65 years old. Don't believe me? Google it. But where is a 20 year old going to get $2000 a year? They get it from cash flow issues by paying their freedom first that's where. $2000 is $40 a week times 50 weeks. Stop wasting money on bad food that will eventually kill you and start paying your freedom first. Stop wasting money on expensive Starbucks coffee and make a whole pot of coffee or tea for a fraction of the price. Quit paying your entertainment first and start paying your freedom first. And consider this, as you set the habits early on, you'll be able to set more than $2000 aside each year. Time is on your side if you're doing the right things. Invest in your F-R-E-E-D-O-M!!!

Another financial planner friend of mine did a great segment on the old radio show that I loved. It was about the concept of opportunity costs. When you invest money (or worse yet spend money) than you lose the opportunity to invest that money in another way. You cost yourself opportunity to have future freedom by spending it now.

His illustration was a real life friend of his that decided to buy his wife a boob job for her birthday to the tune of $10,000. (You may be questioning if the present was for her or him, but that's off track.) My financial planner friend worked up some numbers taking into account that that $10,000 were not being invested in their future freedom and they were only 30 years old. The Rule of 72 and the idea of Opportunity Costs combined showed that boob job of $10,000 was preventing them from having $330,000 later! So he asked if a $330,000 boob job was worth it? Then he explained that he may be incentivizing others to try to steal his wife and did he consider that? Finally, if his friend was dead set on wasting $10,000 at least he could buy something others could enjoy too like a boat or something. That is good radio right there. I don't care who you are.

In the end his friend was not persuaded. I'm telling you, most people are not driven by reason. You must be. Get your budget bucket set up. Get a plan for your freedom and work that plan!

*Real Talk Truth: It's not what you make but what you keep that counts. But it's also what it cost to get it and what you do with it to create your freedom.*

*Whatcha Gonna Do? Begin with the end in mind. Know your numbers and be disciplined with your money. It's not enough to have a plan, you must work the plan. Create your budget now.*

# Chapter 16
# Client Relationship Continued

If you have won all the way around the funnel to this point, it is because you have faithfully worked the top of funnel activities of turning your community into contacts by using media, social media, networking and community service to bring value to your community through your involvement. Then you've been able to connect to contacts and show them why you are the go to agent of choice in your markets and turn them into clients. Then you were great at understanding their motivations and helped your clients to get into the contracts that were best for them. And you smoothly and successfully communicated with everyone just right and got those contracts to close so your clients are happy. Nice job.

Any one transaction can be a tremendous amount of work and you have done it successfully to this point. But your job is not done. Don't stop now. You've got too much invested in this relationship to drop the ball at this point. Now it is time to see all your hard work pay off in a great relationship with a fan of yours. A continued client relationship will help you right back into the community and will get you more contacts!

Continued Client Relationship

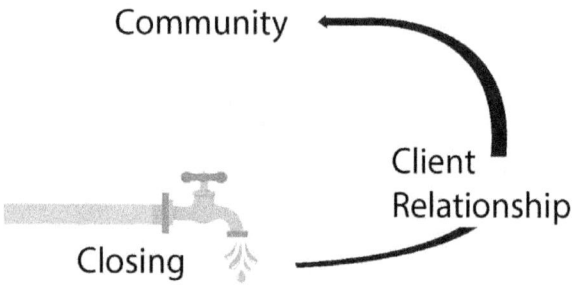

Community

Client
Relationship

Closing

Of course you need to start with the post-closing activity right at the closing table. Take the obligatory smiling picture with the handing of the keys for buyers, or just a picture with the closing packet for the seller. It comes in a title company's branded package, have them hold it up and tag the companies in your postings. They'd be happy to like and share that. Tag the lender too even if you didn't have the buyer. The loan officer will appreciate you and you'll get exposure through their sphere of influence. While you're at it, collect a short video testimony from your client for your website and further social media campaigns.

Hopefully, you're in the habit of giving a closing gift. Maybe you give a nice bottle of wine or a gift card for a restaurant. Do you know off the top of your head what the allowable amount of money for a deduction on a closing gift is? A mere $25. But if you happen to give them a marketing item at the same time, that's a marketing expense not a closing gift. Cutco knives sells agents knives with your logo and contact info engraved on the blade. That makes it a marketing piece they won't ever throw out. The basket that has the wine and cheese can be the closing gift. Imagine their happy surprise to receive such nice items from you right before that picture and video testimony.

If you're working at price points that make sense to do this, you could throw the new buyer a house warming party. Remember all that work you did promoting area restaurants through your blog, social media, radio or TV show? Well revisit those relationships and ask them to cater an event at the new buyer's place at a greatly reduced cost. Give them the chance to leave some of their marketing materials so it is more worthwhile for them. Invite the new neighbors so your clients can get to know their new community. Invite their friends and family so the friends and family get to see the new place. Now the restaurant gets exposure, and more to the point, you are the guy, or gal, that has gone the extra mile and made their housewarming a huge success at no cost to them. No one else at that party had a realtor do anything like that for them. And your client relationship just helped you expand your community.

All that can happen within the first two weeks after closing. Then it's your job to use your CRM to stay connected. Of course you should be sending them your monthly newsletter, but you can also be organizing a quarterly happy hour for clients at a favorite watering hole or an annual party for clients at a bigger venue. One broker I knew did an annual Christmas party. Another one rented out a movie theater for family film night. Certainly tickets to the community theater, the major league baseball team, dinner for two at a local restaurant or any other fun thing can be given away through your monthly newsletter's contest.

At any rate, you will find some of the clients are easier to have relationship with then others. Some of them will love referring you to their community and contacts and will do it many times every year. These relationships need extra attention. Call them once a month just because. Always, and I mean always send them a thank you for every time they mentioned you to a contact of theirs even if it didn't materialize into a new client. Make sure they know you appreciate them.

Others will refer you less often. But they need the same sort of thank you and periodic calls just to check in on them anyway. Don't call to ask them to refer you more, but do call to let them know you are thinking about them. I know social media connections are an easy way to "have friends", but that's nothing compared to saying hi on the phone or grabbing a bite to eat together. Remember you have at least five times a day you could easily socialize with your clients. Don't neglect connecting because they refer only once in a while.

As time goes you'll learn that you can't keep up with every one equally well. Don't feel bad about this. But choose wisely where you spend your time and efforts in building relationships. If they are not going to refer you in the future for whatever reason, keep them on automatic through your CRM's emails and holiday cards. Stay in front of everyone through your use of media and social media, but make sure you call and get face to face with the ones that will refer you. The ones that likely won't refer you for whatever reason can't be your focus. That's fool's gold for sure.

When I started in real estate, more experienced agents told me that all you really need is a database of about 300 past clients. You do a great job staying in touch and they'll use you again when they move again. But we are taking that up several notches by bringing our database the knowledge they need to live well while they are there in the home you sold them and give them reason to keep you top of mind when their sphere of influence has need of a great realtor.

Every trainer you ever had told you what I'm about to tell you. Everyone knows at least 200 people. That, by definition, means that each of the 200 people you know, knows 200 people. What's 200 times 200? Yep, 40,000 people you are one relationship away from all the time. If just 10% of those 40,000 people are thinking of moving in the next year that's 4000 possible clients. If you get just 10% of those deals, hell, if you get just 5% of those deals you'll get 200 new clients in the next year. Do you see the value in continued client relationship?

You need to start now building relationship every way you can. Call your sphere of influence every day you work. Five days a week spend two hours a day systematically calling your people. Don't ask them for referrals. Ask them how they're doing. Ask them if you have the right email and mailing address for them. Ask them about their family, their job, their last vacation. Ask them about their dog. Ask them about them. Show them you care about their well-being. They will ask you about you too. Tell them you are really excited about your work and how you feel you make a difference in people's lives. Show them some of your passion for helping people. Let them know you have some cool media and social media stuff you're excited about sharing with people and ask them to check out your newsletter. Send it to them that day. And then pick up a card and write them a nice note just saying how nice it was to connect with them on the phone.

Let's talk about your monthly e-letter and what needs to be in it. You should have a mobile ready format that lets you stay in touch. Of course there should be a market report section. Let that be a link to your youtube channel where you post several area video reports. In addition there should be a goings on section with all the latest shows coming up. Include music, theater and film. Make sure your best blog articles are highlighted. Have something about buying, selling and investing in real estate. Speaking of investing, make sure you have something from the RICHES acronym in every newsletter too. Maybe you can ask another professional in your referral group to guest write something for that section. An Elder Law attorney, a mortgage broker, an insurance agent or a CPA would all love the chance to show off their expertise in your newsletter. That will give you a chance to deepen your relationship with your professional contacts by featuring them as well.

It sounds like a lot, but remember, you're creating that content as top of funnel activities already. You just need to repurpose it for your newsletter. Once you've got your template figured out, it will take you minutes not hours because the content is complete through your background grind and you just copy and paste your way to a great communication to your people.

The activity of continued client relationship will prove to be the single most important activity in your funnel over time. The point of the Freedom Funnel is to establish a business that doesn't require your 60 hours a week to have contacts, clients, contracts and closings in your community. If you win in the Continued Client Relationship department, it means you've won in every other section first and now have the opportunity to reap the benefits of clients that joyfully and liberally refer you. You can create the sort of business that doesn't have to talk contacts into using your service because their friend, neighbor or family member has done it for you. Your contact to client section becomes scheduling an appointment and signing papers. Nowadays, that can be done via telephone and email. Your biggest problem will be having the time to build relationships with your new clients since the hard work of connecting and persuading them that you are the go to agent in your market is done via referral. If you create a Continued Client Relationship section well you will have a gold mine of referrals. And if you don't do it well, you will effectively collapse the referral gold mine. The job is to build a complete Freedom Funnel and each part of it is a make or break section. The Continued Client Relationship component is no exception.

*Real Talk Truth: The Continued Client Relationship section is the most important in the long run. Most of us don't give it the attention it deserves.*

*Whatcha Gonna Do? Call daily to connect, write notes daily, break bread daily, send monthly e-letter with contests for prizes, have quarterly happy hours at a minimum. Start your continued client relationship at the closing table; don't end it there.*

# Section 3

# The Success

# Chapter 17
# Whatcha Gonna Do?

You have your own story of not making your business what you envision it to be or you wouldn't be reading this book. The system was just laid out for you. The success is entirely up to you. The question is, whatcha gonna do?

I got that question from a Richard Pryor routine where he relays a conversation he had with Jim Brown the NFL great and one of the toughest men of his era. Pryor had much publicized trouble with drug addiction. He famously nearly burned himself to death while free basing cocaine. He was smoking it before there was crack. Jim Brown tried to get him to stop by asking him, "whatcha gonna do Rich, whatcha gonna do?" Pryor, in his hilarious way says the pipe started to try to tell him not to listen to Jim Brown saying no one understood Pryor like the pipe did. But Jim Brown, in his very deep voice just kept asking, "whatcha gonna do?" It's really funny. Youtube it when you get the chance. The addiction of bad behavior versus the undeniable truth that you have the power to change if you will is one of those real talk kind of tragedies that presented correctly make for brilliant comedy. Pryor was above all a brilliant comic but he was also a tragic figure. In no small way, I think we are all both brilliant and tragic in our lives. We have incredible potential for powerful living while at the same time don't do what we need to do to actualize that potential.

So, I ask you the same question Jim Brown asked Richard Pryor, "whatcha gonna do?" Have you, like I have, been humbled enough to decide the time is now? Are you willing to do whatever it takes to get to where you know you should be? Even if it means shooting underhand free throws for all the world to see? (It really isn't as bad as shooting Granny style in front of the entire NBA on TV; I understand it would be remarkably difficult to do that.) You can do this. You just have to make up your mind and start.

Start with your vision. Write out the vision for your business. Not the plan, but the passion for what you want your business and your life to be like. Not the fancy house and cool car vision, but the more meaningful things in life. I told you about my vision for the business in chapter 10.

My vision for my life is simple enough. I've hinted at it all along, but let me state it more succinctly. I want to help people find their way to freedom in their lives. I want it to start with me and mine. I have five children and hope to have grandchildren. I want to tell them the truth about the slanted playing field they play this game of life on. I want them to know they have the power to create the life they want if they are willing to do what it takes to get there. And I want everyone to know that it is solely their responsibility.

I mentioned my daughter's struggles with heroin in chapter 1. She's done very well since then, but every day is another day to win or lose in that struggle. Years ago I packed the kids in a minivan and drove them to a gathering up north of people viewing the Venus Transit. 2012 was the last time the planet Venus was to pass between us and the sun for the next 115 years. I wanted them to see it. It took about seven hours. I have no illusions that the planet moving in front of the sun to the other side somehow changed the nature of things in any metaphysical sense. My interest in showing it to them was more of an object lesson about the fact that circumstances are different every day. Some days you feel good and some days you don't. Some days the boss on the job is in a good mood and some days they are not. Some days the business person you want to do business with is in a no mood and some days they are in a yes mood! Everything is in motion every day. If you're losing today, you can change that tomorrow. But the day after that you'll have to do it again under different circumstances. Today is another opportunity to begin winning again. Whatcha gonna do?

You can imagine that I leaped into action the day I got that call from my daughter in custody. One of the things that action included was intense therapy for not just her, but for her and I together. She needed, and so did I, to have the truth brought out. It included some hard things for me. She looked me in my eye and told me that I had been guilty of shutting her emotions down in my haste to make things "ok" for everyone. She was right. When there are five kids in a blended family setting and four of them are every other week at their mother's place, it was easier to try to sweep things under the rug and try to keep the ship moving ahead even keel. It was easier, but it was the wrong thing to do. One of the main reasons I did it was because I was overworked and stressed about the business. I was chasing the next deal not creating a business that freed me up to be there for her. That is embarrassing and a source of shame in my life, but it is the real talk truth of it.

Where are you failing yourself and the people you care about? What are you going to do about it? I have finally reworked my life to become the person I knew I could be and have the life I knew I wanted. And I still have to do it every day. It was simple, but not easy. Simple because I already knew much of what I should be doing, but not easy because it meant breaking really old patterns that were largely there to make myself feel better about myself even though they caused real problems along the way. My behaviors were more about my insecurities than anything else. They weren't about a well thought out set of actions that created a desirable destiny. Where do you need to change your behaviors?

Consider this as you contemplate that last question: nothing changes without you changing your behaviors. That's point blank and period real talk truth. Remember the discussion about the triangle of feelings, thoughts and actions? It's time to revisit it.

Cognitive Behavioral Triangle

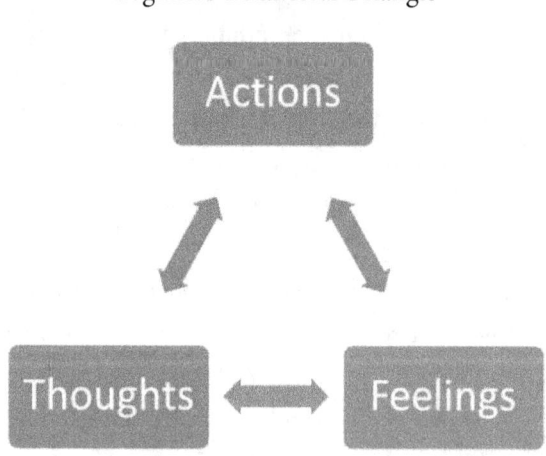

The only place you have power to impact the outcomes in your life is at the top of that triangle. Only your actions impact the outcomes! I don't want to be insensitive when I say I don't care what you think or what you feel about it. Of course your thoughts and feelings are important. But as they relate to outcomes, your thoughts and feelings are only important in so far as they impact your actions. It's your actions alone that determine your outcomes. In that sense, it doesn't matter what you think about it or how you feel about it. It only matters what you do about it.

I played a lot of sports, I coached a lot of sports, I counseled a lot of athletes and coaches as a chaplain over the years. One thing I learned in the process was that as far as the outcomes are concerned, as far as the scoreboard when the clock expires is concerned, the only thing that matters is what you did or didn't do during the competition. And those behaviors were the direct result of what did or didn't do in preparation for the competition. There's an old saying in sports, "you play like you practice so practice like you want to play." If you do what you needed to do in preparation for the competition, then you increase the likelihood of winning. I called it a background grind and a topside hustle. It's not complicated, but it's not easy. However, it's sitting right there for you and I. We simply must find the courage to do it.

So what are you going to do? Start with writing your vision. Then move to assessing your strengths and weaknesses. As you look at The Freedom Funnel, where are you naturally inclined to win and where are you likely to lose? Losing at any section can cost you your freedom. Tell yourself the truth. Ask the people that know you well what they think your strengths and weaknesses are as it relates to The Freedom Funnel. Don't be defensive. Athletes get criticized every day at practice. Coaches wouldn't be doing their jobs if they just told the team that they were good at everything. Such a team would get slaughtered by the teams that told each other the truth and worked on their game together. You need real talk truth, not mealy mouth platitudes.

It is likely that you are one of two kinds of people: you are likely either intuitive in how you do your business and struggle with being systematic, or you are systematic and struggle with being intuitive. Both are necessary. Some sections of The Freedom Funnel lean toward intuition and some toward systemization, but both are necessary in every phase. So as you assess yourself in business, which are you?

The systematic agent that is less intuitive will beat the intuitive agent that is less systematic most every time. But the intuitive agent that gets the right system is unstoppable. You can coach systems a lot easier than you can coach intuition. You can't really make someone that is not intuitive, intuitive. But if they have the right system, they'll get better over time. The system is the key. You've just have to want it bad enough to do what it takes to get it.

You have power! You can get there from here. Whether you believe you have power from the metaphysical Creator, the metaphysical universe or because you have breath in your body still, you have the power to get there.

I mentioned my father was a stroke victim and he worked to rewire his brain and get himself to where he could perform actions again that made his life better. I also mentioned that the stroke caused his doctors to take their eye off the ball in regards to the enlarged prostate he had as a 67 year old. By the time they figured out he was going to survive the stroke and they had better take another look at the prostate, it was too late. The cancer was already in the bone and there was nothing they could do but try to slow down his death. He died almost four years later, in pain, from something called "wasting syndrome." His 6' 1' 230 pound frame was down to about 145 pounds when he died. It's worse than it sounds. But he became the finest man he ever was during my lifetime from a wheelchair and then a bed. He died having taught me more about life in the last months than he did in the entirety of the years before that. It isn't over until it's over. As long as you have breath in your body, you have power. Whatcha gonna do?

It's your actions that matter. It's your actions that change outcomes. I know you won't feel like doing it some days. I know you'll feel out of your comfort zones. Staying in your comfort zones guarantees your failure. Think about it. The Freedom Funnel outline requires that the whole thing is done well because dropping the ball at any one section ruins the experience of your clients and stops the flow of referrals.

You have to work, at least adequately, in areas outside of your comfort zones. No one is good at everything. There are going to be times that you are working at things you are not naturally good at and it is going to be uncomfortable. Do it anyway. Get comfortable with being uncomfortable and do it anyway. Lean on the systemization and automation of The Freedom Funnel and do what you think and feel is hard.

Do it no matter what you think you look like while doing it. Do it no matter how you feel while doing it. Just do it! Shoot granny style anyway (figuratively speaking). In fact, shoot granny style for all the world to see! Because what you choose to do in your background grind and in your topside hustle when the lights are on is the only thing that will change the outcomes. The only question is, whatcha gonna do?

One of the first times I was in a professional football team's practice facility two things really stuck out to me. One was that the food was great which has nothing to do with this, but I'm telling you it was so good I can't think about those experiences without it demanding recognition in my memory. But the other thing was how committed these men were to the process of becoming a great NFL team. It doesn't matter which team facility this took place in because they are all the same. I was to speak to the team, but I spent hours and hours there before the meeting to see them in their work environment and let them see me. I'm a big believer in being real with people. The confessions of failure in this book attest to that. I think the greatest impact is made when we tell the truth. I believe it alone can set us free and freedom is my thing.

I was there early and saw the offensive and defensive lineman lifting weights. They put in incredible work in a matter of one hour. Then they emptied out and a young man who was clearly a back, not a lineman, came in alone. Or, rather, I should say with just one trainer. I figured he was rehabbing from an injury until I saw him put on a mask like a hospital mask. Then he started his workout. After every activity the trainer that was guiding his workout disinfected the barbells or station he was at. It dawned on me he was sick with something and was working hard anyway. He had a game in a few days and he was committed to the background grind of preparation even though his feelings must have been screaming at him to stop. Trust me, he looked miserable. But he was doing everything he could do to prepare to win in spite of those feelings.

When I spoke to the team, he was there in the meeting. Not because I was there, but because it was a team meeting that was going to have preparation for the upcoming game. He sat way in the back away from everyone with his mask in place, but he was there for his meeting with a pen and paper. I changed my entire message that day to talk solely about him. Well, not really about him per se, but he was the illustration to talk about the principle of doing what you are supposed to do no matter how you feel about it.

Everyone in that room knew, from first-hand experience, what I was talking about. They all knew what it is to play hurt, sick, in a bad mood, with things not right and when they were outside of their comfort zones. They all knew what it is to go through the background grind of preparation for the chance to show their topside hustle when the lights came on. They all knew what it takes to be the best, and they all were doing it. I was just there to encourage them. I was just there to let them know they were seen and appreciated. I was just there to acknowledge their hard work and to challenge them to take that same work ethic and vision for their lives beyond the sport of football into their inner lives, into their personal relationships and be prepared to take it into their lives after professional sports. They already knew what it was to work beyond their comfort zones in their careers and were doing it no matter what it took. Whatcha gonna do?

*Real Talk Truth: creating your freedom means being better at things than you have been to date. It probably means doing some things that you have not done because they are out of your comfort zones. Do them anyway.*

*Whatcha Gonna Do? Call your 50 best contacts in this world this week. Write each of them a note using the technique I outlined earlier. Create a campaign for following up buyer and seller leads. Start today and don't quit. Grit matters.*

# Chapter 18
# Behind the Red Door

Here at Red Door we are honest with each other and that works for us. We face the reality of who we are, what we're good at AND what we're not good at. That truth, allows us to figure out how to win with our strengths and beef up our weaknesses so they don't beat us in our businesses. Both of those matter.

It's important to recognize there is more than one way to do this. It's vital that all the sections of The Freedom Funnel are well accounted for. But there is not one way to do that. Everyone is going to do it their own way. At Red Door we work at helping people understand their personality and style. It's important to collaborate and receive coaching with this stuff. I keep saying it because it's true, but no one is good at everything. That's why we need to systematize and staff to our weaknesses. But it's also true that people are good at the same things in different ways.

At Red Door we take a more personalized approach to helping people recognize their own strengths within their own styles. It's very much like coaching sports. One of my daughters played basketball in high school and was a three year varsity starter. She played for a coach that hadn't ever played much basketball himself. But he was a student of the game from his limited perspective. He understood some things about systems. He understood something about the Xs and the Os of basketball. But he didn't understand that certain systems only work with certain players. When you're coaching High School Girl's Basketball you don't get to pick your players. It was the equivalent of trying to put round pegs into square holes. Really good coaches figure out what their players can and can't do and figure out systems that put the players in position to make plays that their players can make. It's a lot more fun that way.

That's what we do at Red Door. We employ assessments and diagnostics to help people win. Trust me it does not let the players off the hook. There are times players in real estate have to make plays that are outside their comfort zones. But those plays are usually more defense than offense. That is to say, those plays are plays that are meant to keep you from losing more than they are plays that are designed to win. We look at strengths and style and find the winning plays too!

## Different Personalities, Different Styles

At Red Door we have three very different people that are all extremely successful. Yours truly, Paul, is one of them. My friend and colleague, Antonio, and the youngest of the three, Mark, are the other two. If you take our first name initials in reverse order you get M.A.P. We're all very different personalities and have very different styles. So we've taken to using the differences to create a map for others by drawing up winning scenarios for the different styles on the varied and complex activities that create wins all the way around The Freedom Funnel.

The Freedom Funnel system is not a one size fits all reality. Mind you the framework is for everyone, but not everyone can do what I do. Of course the reverse is true too. I can't do what everyone can do. No, the key is to face the reality of who we are and who we are not. Then customize the winning plays for who you are. Sounds simple, but it takes some tweaking as you go. That's why professional athletes still practice. I know the great ones make it look easy, but it's only because of the work they put in to be able to do that. Even the best have a slump sometimes and have to go back to the basics to get out of it. No matter the sport or the skill, the player has to feel it for themselves and do it their way. We recognize that at Red Door and help you win your way within the system. It has to be within the system because reality doesn't change. I don't care how you do it, but you have to win at the complex and varied sections that are The Freedom Funnel.

Let me describe briefly the three different personalities that are Mark, Antonio and Paul. Mark is fairly measured and systematic. He thinks it through and writes it down. He's kind of fastidious in his approach to business. Now he is also very good at communicating his thoughts so I don't want you to think he isn't at all intuitive because he is. In fact, he is really quite passionate about it all and it really comes through when he talks. But of the three of us, he is the most organized, deliberate, efficient and steady.

Antonio is organized in his own way. He manages to be effectively involved in a lot of different activities. He has his life and business organized well enough that he is always off on some out of town trip for fun. He is the most gregarious of the three. Antonio talks loud and is a hugger. He laughs loud, he's a practical joker and he likes to needle people. You know the guy. He's forever cracking wise at something. Usually it's pretty funny, but it is almost never measured. He shoots from the hip. He's got a high opinion of his opinions, but he still has sense enough to seek council. He's probably the most organic of the three of us. That is, he is good with the organism that is business. He excels at building relationships.

I, Paul, live at 30,000 feet. I always start with the big picture and try to work my down to earth. Sometimes I don't get there. Theory is everything as far as I am concerned. Creating is far more interesting to me than application. But if you don't apply it, you don't ever make any money at it. So I have to work at seeing it through to completion. From my perspective, I split the difference between organized and organic. The theory is very systematic and takes into account the nature of things. It gives people the sense that I know what I'm talking about. People tend to believe me. On the street, no matter where I am in the world, people ask me for directions. I guess I look like I know where I'm going and that works for me.

You may see yourself in one of these three types, or in some combination of them. It's vital, whoever you are and however you get it done, that you are effective in every section of The Freedom Funnel. There are two main ideas we drive home at Red Door: intuitive and systematic. Put another way, we talk about the organic part of your business and the organization part of your business. The business is the client's experience. Let me say that again another way. You are in the customer service business specializing in the American Dream with an emphasis in housing.

The organic side of that is all about the experience of your clients. Are they getting the level of communication and expert guidance through the home buying and/or selling experience that will make them raving fans at the end? Are they continuing to get great interaction after the closing that builds relationship? That's the organic reality that matters.

The organization side of it is all about maximizing the organic side. Are you on the schedule of activities that allows you to work well in every section of The Freedom Funnel? Do you have the system in place that lets you consistently deliver the experience that builds the relationship in every section? You can. This book's principles applied will do that.

## M.A.P.

MAP here stands for Mark, Antonio and Paul. But it also stands for the fact that there is more than one way to succeed at this. Different personalities use different styles. Let's just take one of the sections of The Freedom Funnel as an example of that. Take the Continued Client Relationship side of things. Mark is great at writing cards and posting to Facebook in a way that his people feel like his people. It is not at all in a shoot from the hip sort of way. It is well planned on a yearly calendar and in his weekly activities. Antonio works the phone and shows up to his circles religiously. He drives further than any of us and uses that time in the car to call people in his sphere. He also has planned out groups he networks like clockwork. Face to face he wins. I use media. I grind on the TV show and turn it into content post production that is blogging material, etc. But it also sets me apart from the crowd really well.

Pick a major and a minor out of the three. Don't try to be all three of the M.A.P. Remember the old saying: Two out of three ain't bad? Well it's true. No one is good at everything. You're going to have to decide what works for you where and when. Sometimes you're going to major on the organic side of things and minor in the organization. Sometimes you'll major on the organization and minor on the organic. Sometimes you'll do it rather like Mark with practical efficiency and craft. Sometimes like Antonio with knee slapping joy and sometimes like Paul with a clarity that persuades. But always you'll do it like you. And that's the key. At Red Door we find out how you win in your business. The framework of The Freedom Funnel gives you the system, but you are the player in this game that has to learn to win your way. We can set you up with winning scenarios, but you have to make the plays.

## Winning Time

When I was 17 years old, I trained for a couple of weeks at a tennis academy in preparation for my freshman year of college where I was on scholarship for tennis. I trained side by side with some great players. One of them won the French Open Doubles Championship and was a long time member of the US Davis Cup Team years later. When I knew him, he was a teenage kid ranked #1 in the world in his age group.

One rainy and humid afternoon we were training indoors and working on our serves side by side. He had a huge serve, but so did I. We were in fact showing off to each other by just bombing serves. I hit one really well and he remarked sarcastically, "can't you hit it any harder?" I chuckled because it was a ridiculously hard serve, but I said, "I don't know. Let's see." Then I unleashed what was one of the nastiest serves I ever hit. I hit it into the ad court to the outside. It landed right on the line. It was crazy big, but the humid day caused my sweaty hand to lose the racket and it flew down into the court about five feet in front of me. The racket hit the court with such force that a chunk of the asphalt court, about the size of a dime, came flying up. Neither of us had ever seen anything like that happen before. I quickly found the chunk of court and replaced it like a divot in golf. We just laughed at how powerful that serve was.

Then I challenged him to top it, and I tried to add some pressure by saying, "ok, match point against you. Whatcha got?" He hauled off and boomed a serve that just barely missed. At that point I told him he should have spun in a first serve to be safe. I'll never forget his response. Mind you this guy became a world class player and earned millions playing on TV during his career. He looked at me just as seriously as a teenager can look and stated as simply as any simple truth I have ever heard by asking, "what good is it to have a big serve if you can't use it when you need it?"

There it is. Win with your strengths. That's what we believe can be done by our people at Red Door. You can win by developing your natural strengths into skills that you can use when you need them. But it is equally important that you strengthen your weaknesses enough through skills, systems and staff so they don't beat you. In order to be able to do these things you and I have to face the truth of who we are and where we're at in our careers. To do that, we need to have the diagnostic tools to assess our situations.

We've developed ways to help people be able to see their situation more clearly. We've also developed the training, tools and systems to help people do something about it. The Freedom Funnel is not just a set of concepts. It's a system to help you win. At Red Door we believe in teamwork AND personal responsibility. That's why I spend time coaching and encouraging our people through the process of building themselves and their businesses into what they want it to be. In turn they build the desired destiny for themselves. It works for us because we have the personnel to execute the plan, and we have the plan. It starts with the people though. You can't coach quality character.

You don't have to be behind the Red Door to benefit from The Freedom Funnel Training. There is a step by step program complete with video tutorials and a workbook like manual to help you build your business using The Freedom Funnel System. It will work you through the original assessments and help you find your way to freedom. There's all the help you need. All you have to do is start and not stop.

Your desired destiny is yours for the taking. You can own your American Dream as in achieve it, if you will own your American Dream as in take personal responsibility for it. That's Michigan Real Talk. Whatcha gonna do?

# Chapter 19
# Q and A with the Author

Q: What makes you qualified to write this book?

A: During the 8 years with Keller Williams I became the top listing agent in the Great Lakes Region. I worked with hundreds of agents that felt alone in the battle and were stumbling through figuring it out. We founded Red Door Realty with a focus on creating a work environment that is actually helpful to agents. We work at real mentoring and developing a collaborative culture that accelerates the learning curve and helps agents succeed.

Q: What makes this role of author and coach worthwhile?

A: Housing is a vital part of everyone's life, and home ownership done right is a foothold into a future financial freedom for most so real estate thrills me. Add to that the chance to coach and mentor agents into accomplishing great things with their business while creating freedom in their lives is a double dip dream come true for me. I've always wanted to make a real difference in people's lives and this role allows me to do that twice over.

Q: What do you think agents should do after reading your book?

A: Reading a book or two doesn't get anyone to change their lives. Coaching does. Everyone who is serious about their business should have one. I have coaches and mentors still. People who realize that reading one book isn't enough may want to talk about next steps for them. They can reach me by email at coaching@OpenRedDoor.com to talk more.